James R. Miller

Silent Times

A Book to help in reading the Bible into Life

James R. Miller

Silent Times
A Book to help in reading the Bible into Life

ISBN/EAN: 9783337171537

Printed in Europe, USA, Canada, Australia, Japan

Cover: Foto ©ninafisch / pixelio.de

More available books at **www.hansebooks.com**

SILENT TIMES:

A Book

TO HELP IN READING THE BIBLE INTO LIFE.

BY

THE REV. J. R. MILLER, D.D.,

AUTHOR OF "WEEK-DAY RELIGION," "HOME-MAKING," "IN HIS STEPS," ETC.

BOSTON:
THOMAS Y. CROWELL & CO.,
1886.

PREFACE.

The point at which many Christians fail in the using of divine truths is the point at which doctrine should be transmuted into life. They know and honor the Bible as the word of God, and sincerely wish to conform their lives to its inspired teachings, but have difficulty in applying them to the actual experiences of daily life. This book is offered as a humble help in this direction. Its aim is to bring the divine lessons down, and give some hints of the way they may be used on common days and in the actual experiences of those days. The title, "Silent Times," is suggestive of the need of seasons of quiet in every life that would grow into full, rich beauty. It is suggestive also of one particular use that may be made of the book, — the reading of its chapters, or portions of them, in the "silent times" of busy, feverish days, as helps in the direction of true Christian growth. The book is sent out in Christ's name, and with the hope that it may make the way a little plainer for some earnest pilgrims, and religion a little more real, and that it may become a lamp for some dark ways, and a staff for some rough and steep paths.

J. R. M.

PHILADELPHIA.

CONTENTS.

CHAPTER		PAGE
I.	Silent Times	7
II.	Personal Friendship with Christ	17
III.	Having Christ in Us	29
IV.	Copying but a Fragment	41
V.	Thy Will, not Mine	52
VI.	God's Reserve of Goodness	62
VII.	The Blessing of Not Getting	73
VIII.	"Afterward"	84
IX.	The Blessedness of Longing	93
X.	The Cost and Worth of Sympathy	102
XI.	Finding One's Mission	112
XII.	Living up to our Best Intentions	123
XIII.	Life's Double Ministry	134
XIV.	The Ministry of Well-wishing	145
XV.	Helping without Money	156
XVI.	Timeliness in Duty	171
XVII.	The Office of Consoler	181
XVIII.	Living by the Day	191
XIX.	Habits in Religious Life	200
XX.	The Power of the Tongue	213
XXI.	The Home Conversation	223
XXII.	An Old Bible Portrait	234
XXIII.	Sorrow in Christian Homes	243
XXIV.	Dealing with Our Sins	254

SILENT TIMES.

CHAPTER I.

SILENT TIMES.

IN Wellesley College a special feature of the daily life of the household is the morning and evening "silent time." Both at the opening and closing of the day, there is a brief period, marked by the strokes of a bell, in which all the house is quiet. Every pupil is in her room. There is no conversation. No step is heard in the corridors. The whole great house with its thronging life is as quiet as if all its hundreds of inmates were sleeping. There is no positively prescribed way of spending these silent minutes in the rooms, but it is understood that all whose hearts so incline them shall devote the time to devotional reading, meditation, and prayer. At least, the design of establishing this period of quiet as part of the daily life of the school, is to give opportunity for such devotional exercises, and by its solemn hush to suggest to all the fitness, the helpfulness, and the need of such periods of communion with God. The bell that calls for silence, also calls to thought and prayer; and even the most indifferent must be affected by its continual recurrence.

Every true Christian life needs its daily "silent times," when all shall be still, when the busy activity of other hours shall cease, and when the heart, in holy hush, shall commune with God. One of the greatest needs in Christian life in these days is more devotion. Ours is not an age of prayer so much as an age of work. The tendency is to action rather than to worship; to busy toil rather than to quiet sitting at the Saviour's feet to commune with him. The key-note of our present Christian life is consecration, which is understood to mean devotion to active service. On every hand we are incited to work. Our zeal is stirred by every inspiring incentive. The calls to duty come to us from a thousand earnest voices.

And this is well. There is little fear that we shall ever grow too earnest in working for our Master, or that our enthusiasm in his service shall ever become too intense. We are set on earth to toil for the world's good and for God's glory. The day's heat is not to draw us from our active duty. Till death comes, as God's messenger to call us from toil, we are not to seek to be freed from service. Devotion is not all. Peter wished to stay on the Mount of Transfiguration, to go back no more to the cold, sin-stricken world below; but no: down at the mountain's base, human suffering and sorrow were waiting for the coming of the Healer, and the Master and his disciples must leave the rapture of heavenly communion, and hasten down to carry healing and comfort. It is always so. While we enjoy the blessedness of fellowship with God in the closet, there come in at our closed doors, and break upon our ears, the cries of human need and sorrow outside. Amid the raptures of devotion we hear the calls of duty waiting without. We should never allow our ecstasies of spiritual enjoyment to make us forgetful of the needs of others around us. Even the Mount of Transfiguration must not hold us away from ministry.

The truest religious life is one whose devotion gives food and strength for service. The way to spiritual health lies in the paths of consecrated activity. It is related in monastic legends of St. Francesca, that although she was unwearied in her devotions, yet if during her prayers she was summoned away by any domestic duty, she would close her book cheerfully, saying that a wife and a mother, when called upon, must quit her God at the altar to find him in her domestic affairs. Yet the other side is just as true. Before there can be a strong, vigorous, healthy tree, able to bear much fruit, to stand the storm, to endure the heat and cold, there must be a well-planted and well-nourished root; and before there can be a prosperous, noble, enduring Christian life in the presence of the world, safe in temptation, unshaken in trials, full of good fruits, perennial and unfading in its leaf, there must be a close walk with God in secret. We must receive from God before we can give to others, for we have nothing of our own with which to feed men's hunger or quench their thirst. We are but empty vessels at the best, and must wait to be filled before we have any thing to carry to those who need. We must listen at heaven's gates before we can go out to sing the heavenly songs in the ears of human weariness and sorrow. Our lips must be touched with a coal from God's altar before we can become God's messengers to men. We must lie much upon Christ's bosom before our poor earthly lives can be struck through with the spirit of Christ, and made to shine in the transfigured beauty of his blessed life. Devotion is never to displace duty, — it often brings new duties to our hands, — but it fits us for activity.

> "That Thy full glory may abound, increase,
>   And so Thy likeness shall be formed in me,
> I pray: the answer is not rest or peace,
> But charges, duties, wants, anxieties,
>   Till there seems room for every thing but Thee,
> And never time for any thing but these.

The busy fingers fly; the eyes may see
  Only the glancing needle which they hold:
But all my life is blossoming inwardly,
And every breath is like a litany;
  While through each labor, like a thread of gold,
Is woven the sweet consciousness of Thee."

In order to this preparation for usefulness and service, we all need to get into the course of our lives many quiet hours, when we shall sit alone with Christ in personal communion with him, listening to his voice, renewing our wasted strength from his fulness, and being transformed in character by looking into his face. Busy men need such quiet periods of spiritual communion; for their days of toil, care, and struggle tend to wear out the fibre of their spiritual life, and exhaust their inner strength. Earnest women need such silent times, for there are many things in their daily household life and social life to exhaust their supplies of grace. The care of their children, the very routine of their home-life, the thousand little things that try their patience, vex their spirits, and tend to break their calm; the influences of much of their social life, with its manifold temptations to artificialness, insincerity, formality, unreality, or, on the other hand, to frivolity, idleness, vanity, and worldliness, — amid all these distracting, dissipating, secularizing influences, every earnest woman needs to get into her life at least one quiet hour every day, when, like Mary, she can wait at the feet of Jesus, and have her own soul calmed and fed.

Preachers, teachers, Christian workers, all need the same. How can men stand in the Lord's house to speak his words to the people unless they have first waited at Christ's feet to get their message? How can any one teach the children the truths of life without having been himself freshly taught of God? How can any one bear heavenly gifts to needy souls if he has not been at the Lord's treasure-house to get these gifts? Dr. Austin Phelps, in speaking of the danger of incessant Christian activity without a corresponding secret life with God, says, "The very obvious peril is, that the vitality of holiness may be exhausted by inward decay through the want of an *increase* of its devotional spirit proportioned to the expansion of its active forces. Individual experience may become shallow for the want of meditative habits and much communion with God. Activity can never sustain *itself*. Withdraw the vital force which animates and propels it, and it falls like a dead arm. We cannot, then, too keenly feel, each one for himself, that a still and secret life with God must energize all holy duty, as vigor in every fibre of the body must come from the strong, calm, faithful beat of the heart."

A Christian man of intense business enterprise and activity was laid aside by sickness. He who never would intermit his labors was compelled to come to a dead halt. His restless limbs were stretched motionless on the bed. He was so weak that he could scarcely utter a word. Speaking to a friend of the contrast between his condition now and when he had been driving his immense business, he said, "Now I am *growing*. I have been running my soul thin by my activity. Now I am growing in the knowledge of myself and of some things which most intimately concern me." No doubt there are many of us who are running our souls thin by our incessant action, without finding quiet hours for feeding and waiting upon God.

> " The world is too much with us : late and soon,
>   Getting and spending, we lay waste our powers.
> Little we see in nature that is ours :
>   We have given our souls away, a sordid boon."

Blessed, then, is sickness or sorrow or any experience that compels us to stop, that takes the work out of our hands for a little season, that empties our hearts of their thousand cares, and turns them toward God to be taught of him.

But why should we wait for sickness or sorrow to *compel* into our lives these necessary quiet hours? Would it not be far better for us to train ourselves to go apart each day for a little season from the noisy, chilling world, to look into God's face and into our own hearts, to learn the things we need so much to learn, and to draw secret strength and life from the fountain of life in God? George Herbert's quaint lines contain wise counsel: —

"By all means use sometimes to be alone;
   Salute thyself, see what thy soul doth wear.
Dare to look in thy closet, — for 'tis thine own, —
   And tumble up and down what thou findest there."

With these sacred "silent times" in every day of toil and struggle, we shall be always strong, and "prepared unto every good work." Waiting thus upon God, we shall daily renew our wasted strength, and be able to run and not be weary, to walk and not be faint, and to mount up with wings as eagles in bold spiritual flights.

CHAPTER II.

PERSONAL FRIENDSHIP WITH CHRIST.

> "I would converse with Thee from day to day,
> With heart intent on what Thou hast to say,
> And through my pilgrim-walk, whate'er befall,
> Consult with Thee, O Lord! about it all.
> Since Thou art willing thus to condescend
> To be my intimate, familiar friend,
> Oh! let me to the great occasion rise,
> And count Thy friendship life's most glorious prize!"

WE are in danger on several sides of superficial and shallow conceptions of a religious life. One of these is, that it consists in correct doctrinal beliefs, that holding firmly and intelligently to the truths of the gospel about Christ makes one a Christian. Another is the liturgical, that the faithful observance of the forms of worship is the essential element in a Christian life. Still another is, that conduct is all, that Christianity is but a system of morality. Then, even among those who fully accept the doctrine of Christ's atonement for sin, there is ofttimes an inadequate conception of the life of faith, a dependence for salvation upon one great past act of Christ, — his death, — without forming with him a personal relation as a present, living Saviour. In the New Testament the Christian's relation to Christ is represented as a personal acquaintance with him, which ripens into a close and tender friendship. This was our Lord's own ideal of discipleship. He invited men to come to him, to break other ties, and attach themselves personally to him; to leave all and go with him. He claimed the full allegiance of men's hearts and lives: he must be first in their affections, and first in their obedience and service. He offered himself to men, not merely as a helper from without, not merely as one who would save them by taking their sins and dying for them, but as one who desired to form with them a close, intimate, and indissoluble friendship. It was not a tie of duty merely, or of obligation, or of doctrine, or of cause, by which he sought to bind his followers to himself, but a tie of personal friendship.

That which makes one a Christian is not therefore the acceptance of Christ's teachings, the uniting with his church, the adoption of his morals, the espousing of his cause, but the receiving of him as a personal Saviour, the entering into a covenant of eternal friendship with him. We are not saved by a creed, which gathers up in a few golden sentences the essence of the truth about Christ's person and work: we must have the Christ himself whom the creed holds forth in his radiant beauty and grace. We are in the habit of saying that Christ saved us by dying for us on the cross. In an important sense, this is true. We never could have been saved if he had not died for us. But we are actually saved by our relation to a living, loving, personal Saviour, into whose hands we commit all the interests of our lives, and who becomes our friend, our helper, our keeper, our care-taker, our all in all. Christian faith is not merely laying our sins on the Lamb of God and trusting to his one great sacrifice: it is the laying of ourselves on the living, loving heart of one whose friendship becomes thenceforward the sweetest joy of our lives.

The importance of this personal knowledge of Christ is seen when we think of him as the revealer of the Father. The disciples first learned to know Christ in his disguise, with his divine glory veiled. He led them on, talking to them, walking with them, winning their confidence and their love, and at length they learned that the Being who had grown so inexpressibly dear to them was the manifestation of God himself, and that by their relation to him as his friends, their poor, sinful humanity was lifted up into union with the Father. They became children of God through their attachment to the only-begotten Son of God. Clinging to him, and cleaving to him in deathless friendship, in his humiliation, he exalted them in his exaltation to be joint-heirs with him in his divine inheritance. It was as if a royal prince should leave his father's palace for a time, and in disguise dwell among the plain people as one of themselves, winning their love, and binding them to him in strong personal friendship, and then, disclosing his royalty, should lead them to his palace, and keep them about him ever after as his friends and brothers, sharing his rank and honors with them. The friends Christ won in his lowly condescension he did not cast off when he went back to his glory: he lifted them up with him to share his heavenly blessedness.

It is in the same way that Christ now saves men. He wins their love and trust by the manifestation of his love for them, and then exalts them to the possession of the privileges which belong to himself as the Son of God. Any one whose life is knit to Christ in love and faith, is lifted up into the family of God. Some one has represented this truth in this way: A vine has been torn from the tree on which it grew and clung, and lies on the ground: it never can lift itself up again to its place. Then the tree bends down low until it touches the earth. The vine unclasps its tendrils which have twined about frail and unworthy weeds, and, feebly reaching upward, fixes them upon the tree's strong, living branches. The tree, again lifting itself up, carries the vine with it to its natural and original place of beauty and fruitfulness, where it shares the tree's glory. This is a parable of soul-history. We were torn from our place, and lay perishing in our sins, clinging to the earth's treacherous trusts. We could never lift ourselves up to God. Then God himself stooped down in the incarnation, bending low to touch these souls of ours; and when our hearts let go earth's sins and its frail, false trusts, and lay hold never so feebly, by the tendrils of faith and love, upon Christ, we are lifted up, and become children and heirs of God.

But how may we form a personal acquaintance with Christ? It was easy enough for John and Mary, and the others who knew him in the flesh. His eyes looked into theirs; they heard his words; they sat at his feet, or leaned upon his bosom. We cannot know Christ in this way, for he is gone from earth; and we ask how it is possible for us to have more than a biographical acquaintance with him. If he were a mere man, nothing more than this would be possible. It were absurd to talk about knowing St. John personally, or forming an intimate friendship with St. Paul. We may learn much of the character of these men from the fragments of their story which are preserved in the Scriptures, but we can never become personally acquainted with them until we meet them in the other world. With Christ, however, it is different. The Church did not lose him when he ascended from Olivet. He never was more really in the world than he is now. He is as much to those who love him and believe on him as he was to his friends in Bethany. He is a present, living Saviour; and we may form with him an actual relation of personal friendship, which will grow closer and tenderer as the years go on, deepening with each new experience, shining more and more in our hearts, until at last, passing through the portal which men misname death, but which really is the beautiful gate of life, we shall see him face to face, and know him even as we are known.

Is it possible for all Christians to attain this personal, conscious intimacy with Christ? There are some who do not seem to realize it.

To them Christ is a creed, a rule of life, an example, a teacher, but not a friend. There are some excellent Christians who seem to know Christ only biographically. They have no experimental knowledge of him: he is to them at best an absent friend, — living, faithful, and trusted, but still absent. No word of discouragement, however, should be spoken to such. The Old Testament usually goes before the New, in experience as well as in the biblical order. Most Christians begin with the historical Christ, knowing *of* him before they know *him*. Conscious personal intimacy with him is ordinarily a later fruit of spiritual growth; yet it certainly appears from the Scriptures that such intimacy is possible to all who truly believe in Christ. Christ himself hungers for our friendship, and for recognition by us, and answering affection from us; and if we take his gifts without himself and his love, we surely rob ourselves of much joy and blessedness.

The way to this experimental knowledge of Christ is very plainly marked out for us by our Lord himself. He says that if we love him, and keep his words, he will manifest himself unto us, and he and his Father will come and make their abode with us. It is in loving him, and doing his will, that we learn to know Christ; and we learn to love him by trusting him. A dying youth looked up into the face of a friend, and with troubled tones said, "I want to love Christ: will you tell me how?"—"Trust him first," was the answer, "and you will learn to love him without trying at all." It was a new revelation. "I always thought I must love Christ before I could have any right to trust him," was the answer. Ofttimes we learn to know our human friends by trusting them. We see no special beauty or worth in them as they move by our side in the ordinary experiences of life: but we pass at length into circumstances of trial, where we need friendship; and then the noble qualities of our friends appear, as we trust them, and they come nearer to us, and prove themselves true. In like manner, most of us really get acquainted with Christ only in experiences of need, in which his love and faithfulness are revealed.

The value of a personal acquaintance with Christ is incalculable. There are men and women whom it is worth a great deal to have as friends. As our intimacy with them ripens, their lives open out like sweet flowers, disclosing rich beauty to our sight, and pouring fragrance upon our spirits. A true and great friendship is one of earth's richest and best blessings. It is ever breathing songs into our hearts, kindling aspirations and hopes, starting impulses of good, teaching holy lessons, and shedding all manner of benign influences upon our lives. But the friendship of Christ does infinitely more than this for us. It purifies our sinful lives; it makes us brave and strong; it inspires us ever to the best and noblest service. Its influence, perpetually brooding over us, woos out the winsomest graces of mind and spirit. The richest, the sweetest, and the only perennial and never failing, fountain of good in this world, is the personal, experimental knowledge of Christ.

That Christ should condescend thus to give to us sinful men his pure, divine friendship is the greatest wonder of the world; but there is no doubt of the fact. No human friendship can ever be half so close and intimate as that which the lowliest of us may enjoy with our Saviour. If we but realize our privileges, the enriching that will come to our lives through this glorious relationship will be better than all gold and gems.

> "And can a thing so sweet,
> And can such heavenly condescension, be?
> Ah! wherefore tarry thus our lingering feet?
>   It can be none but Thee.
>
> There is the gracious ear
> That never yet was deaf to sinner's call:
> We will not linger, and we dare not fear,
>   But kneel, and tell Thee all.
>
> We tell Thee of our sin,
> Only half loathed, only half wished away;
> And those clear eyes of love that look within,
>   Rebuke us, seem to say,—
>
> 'Oh! bought with My own blood,
> Mine own, for whom My precious life I gave,
> Am I so little prized, remembered, loved,
>   By those I died to save?'

And under that deep gaze
Sorrow awakes. We kneel with eyelids wet,
And marvel, as with Peter at the gate,
  That we could so forget.

We tell Thee of our care,
Of the sore burden pressing day by day;
And in the light and pity of Thy face
  The burden melts away.

We breathe our secret wish,
The importunate longing which no man may see:
We ask it humbly, or, more restful still,
  We leave it all to Thee.

The thorns are turned to flowers;
All dark perplexities seem light and fair;
A mist is lifted from the heavy hours,
  And Thou art everywhere."

CHAPTER III.

HAVING CHRIST IN US.

"As some rare perfume in a vase of clay
  Pervades it with a fragrance not its own,
So when Thou dwellest in a mortal soul,
  All heaven's own sweetness seems around it thrown."

THE Scriptures make a great deal of having Christ in men, if they are Christians. Christ himself speaks of abiding in his people, and of his life as flowing through them as the life of the vine flows through its branches. The figure of the body is used, believers being members of Christ's body, and deriving all their life from him. The idea of a building or temple with the divine Spirit as indwelling guest, is also employed to represent the Christian's relation to his Lord. Then, St. Paul says without figure, " Christ liveth in me," and speaks of being "filled with the Spirit," "filled with all the fulness of God," as a possible and most desirable attainment of Christian experience. From the many forms in which this truth is represented in the Scriptures, it is evident that the ideal Christian life is one that is thoroughly pervaded, saturated, so to speak, with the life and spirit of Christ. Far more certainly is implied than mere divine influence over us or upon us from without, such influence as a friend exerts over a friend, a teacher over a pupil, or even a mother over a child. To become a Christian is to have a new spiritual life enter the soul, as when a seed with its living germ is planted in the dead soil: to grow as a Christian is to have this new life increase in strength and energy, making daily conquests over the old nature, extending itself, and expelling the evil by the force of its own good, and ultimately bringing the affections, feelings, desires, and all the activities, even the thoughts of the heart, into subjection to Christ.

There is a great difference between having Christ outside and having him in us. If he is only outside, we may listen for his words, and try to obey his voice, following where he leads;

and we may gaze upon his loveliness, and seek to copy it in our lives; but our following and obeying will be under the impulse of duty only, with no inward constraint; and our striving after the divine likeness will be like the carving of a figure in cold marble rather than the growing up of a life from within by its own vital force and energy into fulness of power and beauty.

Only as we get Christ into our hearts, and let him dwell in us by his Spirit, shall we reach the true ideal of Christian life and experience. Then shall we do right, not by direction of written rule, but by the promptings of our regenerated nature, the Christ indwelling. Then shall our dull lives be transfigured by the light that shines in our hearts, and slowly changes all the earthliness to heavenliness. Then shall the features of the divine image come out little by little as the new life within forces itself through the dull crust of the old nature, until at length the full beauty of Christ shines where once only sin's marred visage was seen.

Christ within makes an inner joy that all the darkness of earth's trials cannot quench.

There are great diversities of experience in sorrow. Some when this world's lights are quenched are left in utter gloom, like a house without lamp or candle or flickering firelight when the sun goes down. Others, in similar darkness, stand radiant in the deep shadows: they have bright light within themselves. Christ dwells in them, and the beams from his blessed life turn night into day. There is an ancient picture of the Christ-child in the stable which illustrates this experience. The child lies upon the straw, the mother is bending over him, the wondering shepherds are near, and in the background are the cattle. It is night, and there is only one feeble lantern in the place; but from the infant child a radiance streams which lights up all the rude scene. So it is in sorrow-darkened hearts when Christ truly dwells within. The light streaming from him who is the light of the world, in whom is no darkness, illumines all the gloom of grief. Indeed, when Christ dwells in the heart, sorrow is a blessing, because it reveals beauties and joys which could not have been seen in the earthly light. It is one of the blessings of night, that without it we could never see the stars : it is one of the blessings of trial, that without it we could never see the precious comforts of God.

> "Were there no night, we could not read the stars,
>   The heavens would turn into a blinding glare ;
> Freedom is best seen through prison-bars,
>   And rough seas make the haven passing fair ;
> We cannot measure joys but by their loss ;
>   When blessings fade away, we see them then ;
> Our richest clusters grow around the cross,
>   And in the night-time angels sing to men."

When Christ is within us, sorrow is a time of revelation. It is like the cloud that crowned the summit of the holy mountain into which Moses climbed, and by which he was hidden so long from the eyes of the people. While folded in the clouds, he was looking upon God's face. Sorrow's cloud hides the world, and wraps the wondering one in thick darkness ; but in the darkness, Christ himself unveils the splendor and glory of his face. There are many who never saw the beauty of Christ, and never knew him in the intimacy of a personal friendship, till they saw him, and learned to talk with him as friend with friend, in the hour of sorrow's darkness. When the lamps of earth went out, Christ's face appeared.

But Christ is not a friend for sorrow alone. We do not have to wait till trial comes to enjoy his love, and be blessed by his indwelling. His light shines in many places where the brightness of other lamps still beams. Yet, even there, it does not shine in vain. Christ within has a deep meaning to the joyous as well as to the sad. All blessings are richer, all gladness is sweeter, all love is purer, because we have Christ. Peace in the heart makes every earthly beauty lovelier. Indeed, all human gladness is but a vanishing picture, a passing illusion, unless the joy of the Lord be its spring and source.

What confidence it gives to us in our enjoyment of the transient and uncertain things of earth, to know that these are not our only possessions; that if we lose them, we shall still be rich and secure, because we shall still have

Christ. All day the stars are in the sky. We cannot see them in the glare of the sunshine; but it is something, surely, to know that they are there, and that, when it grows dark, they will shine out. So, amid abounding human joy, it is a precious confidence to know that there are divine comforts veiled, invisible to our eyes in the sunshine about us, which will flash out the moment the earthly joy is darkened.

> "I wonder if the world is full
> Of other secrets beautiful,
> As little guessed, as hard to see,
> As this sweet, starry mystery?
> Do angels veil themselves in space,
> And make the sun their hiding-place?
> Do white wings flash as spirits go
> On heavenly errands to and fro,
> While we, down-looking, never guess
> How near our lives they crowd and press?
> If so, at life's set we may see
> Into the dusk steal noiselessly
> Sweet faces that we used to know,
> Dear eyes like stars that softly glow,
> Dear hands stretched out to point the way, —
> And deem the night more fair than day."

To the happiest heart that really makes room for Christ within, there is always the assurance of a world of spiritual blessings, hopes, and joys, lying concealed in the lustre of human gladness, like stars in the noonday sky, but ready to pour their brightness upon us the moment the night falls with its shadows. Whether, therefore, the earthly light be bright or dark, Christ in the heart gives great blessedness and peace.

But there is another way in which Christ within us will be made manifest. If we have this divine indwelling, we should also have in ever-increasing measure in all our life the gentle and loving Spirit of the Master. We should not claim to have Christ in us, if, in our conduct and speech, in our disposition and temper, and in our relations with our fellow-men, there is none of the mind of Christ. If Christ truly be in us, he cannot long be hidden in our hearts without manifestation, but there will be a gradual transformation of our outer life into Christlikeness. As he lived, we will live; as he ministered to others, we will minister; as he was holy, we will be holy; as he was patient, thoughtful, unselfish, gentle, and kind, so will we be. Christ came to our world to pour divine kindness on weary, needy, perishing human lives. Christ truly in our hearts should send us out on the same mission. And there is need everywhere for love's ministry. The world to-day needs nothing more than true Christlikeness in those who bear Christ's name, and represent him. Christ went about doing good: he sought to put hope and cheer into all he met. If Christ be in us, we should strive to perpetuate this Christ-ministry of love in this world. Hearts are breaking with sorrow, men are bowing under burdens too heavy for them, duty is too large, the battles are too hard: it is our mission, if Christ be in us, to do for these weary, overwrought, defeated, and despairing ones what Christ himself would do if he were standing where we stand. He wants us to represent him; and he fills us with his Spirit, that we may be able to scatter the blessings of helpfulness and gladness all about us. Yet, one of the saddest things about life is, that, with so much power to help others by kindliness of word and kindliness of act, many of us pass through the world in silence or with folded hands. Silence has ofttimes a better ministry than speech. It were well very frequently if we did not speak where now we speak with quick and glib tongue. There are words that pain and wound the heart. There is speech that is most cruel. There are tongues that had better been born dumb than to have the gift of speech, and employ it as they do. "Speech is silvern, silence is golden," says the old proverb; and there are homes and lives in which it were well if fewer words were uttered. But there are also silences that are cruel. We walk beside our friends whose hearts are heavy, who are bearing burdens that well-nigh crush them, who are yearning for cheer and sympathy and love : we talk incessantly with them of other things, — of business, of society, of books, of a thousand things, — but never speak the sweet word for which they are hungering. If the Spirit of Christ is in us, it should prompt us to speak such words as Christ himself would speak if he were in our place.

Surely we should learn the lesson of gentle, thoughtful kindness to those we love, and to all we meet in life's busy ways; and we should show the kindness, too, while their tired feet walk in life's toilsome paths, and not wait to bring flowers for their coffins, or to speak words of cheer when their ears are closed, and their hearts are stilled, and it is too late to give them comfort and joy.

If we have the true Christ-spirit in our hearts, it will work out in transfigured life and in Christly ministry; it will lead to the brightening of one little spot, at least, on this big earth. There are a few people whom God calls to do great things for him; but the best things most of us can do in this world is just to live out a real, simple, consecrated, Christian life in our allotted place. Thus, in our little measure, we shall repeat the life of Christ himself, showing men some feeble reflection of his sweet and loving face, and doing in our poor way a few of the beautiful things he would do if he were here himself. Whittier tells us, —

> "The dear Lord's best interpreters
> Are humble, human souls:
> The gospel of a life
> Is more than books or scrolls."

CHAPTER IV.

COPYING BUT A FRAGMENT.

"Heaven whispers wisdom to the wayside flower,
Bidding it use its own peculiar dower,
And bloom its best within its little span.
We must each do not what we will, but can,
Nor have we duty to exceed our power."

NOTHING is more striking to a close observer of human life than the almost infinite variety of character which exists among those who profess to be Christians. No two are alike. Even those who are alike revered for their saintliness, who alike seem to wear the image of their Lord, whose lives are alike attractive in their beauty, show the widest diversity in individual traits, and in the cast and mould of their character. Yet all are sitting before the same model; all are striving after the same ideal; all are imitators of the same blessed life. There is but one standard of true Christian character, — the likeness of Christ. It is into his image that we are all in the end to be transformed, and it is toward his holy beauty that we are always to strive. We are to live as he lived: we are to copy his features into our lives. Wherever, in all the world, true disciples of Christ are found, they are trying to reproduce in themselves the likeness of their Master.

Why is it, then, that there is such variety of character and disposition among those who aim to follow the same example? Why are not all just alike? If a thousand artists were to paint the picture of the same person, their pictures, if faithful, would show the same features. But a thousand persons seek to copy into their own lives the likeness of Christ, and the result is a thousand different representations of that likeness, no two the same. Why is there this strange diversity in Christian lives, when all have before them the same original type?

One reason for this is that God does not bestow upon all his children the same gifts, the same natural qualities. The Creator loves variety, as all his works attest: no two animals are precisely alike in every feature; no two plants are exactly similar in their structure; no two human lives in all the race are identical in all respects; and divine grace does not recast all dispositions in the same mould. When gold is minted, each coin of a kind is stamped by the same die; and a million coins of the same value will all be precisely alike. But life is not minted as gold is. Grace does not transform Peter into a John, nor Paul into a Barnabas, nor Luther into a Melanchthon. Regeneration does not make busy, bustling Martha quiet and reposeful, like her sister Mary; nor does it change Mary's calm, restful spirit into the anxious and distracted activity of Martha. It makes them both friends of Jesus, devoted to him in love and loyalty and service; but it leaves each of them herself in all her individual characteristics. It makes them both like Christ in holiness, in consecration, in heavenly longings; but it does not touch those features which give to each one her personal identity.

You drop twenty different seeds in the same garden-bed, and they spring up into twenty different kinds of plants, from the delicate mignonette to the flaunting sunflower. No skill of gardening can make all the plants alike. The fuchsia will always be a fuchsia, the rose will always be a rose, the geranium will always be a geranium. In the same soil, with the same sunshine and rain, and the same culture, each grows up after its kind. In like manner divine grace does not make all Christian women either Marys or Marthas, or Dorcases or Priscillas, nor all Christian men either Johns or Peters, or Barnabases or Aquilas; but each believer grows up into his own peculiar self. Regeneration neither adds to nor takes from our natural gifts; and since there is infinite variety in the endowments and qualities originally bestowed upon different individuals, there is the same variety in the company of Christ's followers.

Another reason for this diversity among Christians is because even the best and holiest saints realize but a little of the image of Christ, have only one little fraction and fragment of his likeness in their souls. In one of his followers, there is some one feature of Christ's blessed life that appears; in another, there is another feature; in a third, still a different feature. One seeks to copy Christ's gentleness, another his patience, another his sympathy, another his meekness. A thousand believers may all, in a certain sense, be like Christ, and yet no two of them have, or consciously strive after, just the same features of Christ in their souls. The reason is, that the character of Christ is so great, so majestic, so glorious, that it is impossible to copy all of it into any one little human life; and again, each human character is so imperfect and limited, that it cannot reach out in all directions after the boundless and infinite character of Christ.

It is as if a great company of artists were sent to paint each one a picture of the Alps. Each chooses his own point of observation, and selects the particular feature of the Alps he desires to paint. They all bring back their pictures; but lo! no two of them are alike.

One canvas presents a sweet valley-scene, with its quiet stream and bright flowers; another has for its central figure a wild crag among the clouds; another a snow-crowned peak, glittering in the sunshine; another a rushing torrent leaping over the rocks; another a mighty glacier. Yet no one of the artists can say that the pictures of the others are not true. They are probably as true as his own, but there is not one of them all that has painted the whole Alps. Each one has put upon his canvas only the little part of the magnificent scene which he saw.

So it is with those who are striving to reproduce the likeness of Christ in their own lives. A thousand Christians, earnest and sincere, begin to follow him and to imitate him. One seizes upon one feature which to him seems to be the central beauty of Christ's character; another, looking upon the same glorious person with different eyes, or from the view-point of different experiences, sees another feature altogether, and calls it Christ; each one strives to copy the particular elements of Christly character which he sees. No two reproductions are precisely the same : no two have the same conception of Christlikeness. Yet no one can say that the others are not true Christians, that they have not also seen the Lord, and have not faithfully copied into their own lives what they saw of him.

The truth is, the Alps as a whole are too varied, too vast, for any one artist to take into his perspective, and paint upon his canvas. The best he can do is to portray some one or two features, — the features his eye can see from where he stands. And Christ is too great in his infinite perfections, in the majestic sweep of his character, in the many-sidedness of his beauty, for any one of his finite followers to copy the whole of his image into his own little life. The most that any of us can do is to get into our own soul one little fragment of the wonderful likeness of our Lord.

Thus it is that there is such variety in the individual dispositions of Christians, while all seek to follow the same copy, and while all may be equally faithful in their noble endeavors.

The practical lesson from this fact is, that no one follower of Christ should condemn another because the other's spiritual life is not of the same stamp as his own. Let not Martha, busied with her much serving, running everywhere to missionary meetings, or to visit the sick and the poor, find fault with Mary in her quiet devotion, peaceful, thoughtful, gentle, loving, because she does not abound in the same activities. Nor let Mary in her turn judge Martha, and call her piety superficial. Let her honor it rather as the copy of another feature of the infinite loveliness of Christ.

There is the greatest diversity in the modes of service rendered by different followers of Christ. All may be alike loyal and acceptable, and yet no two be the same. Each follows Christ along his own path, and does his work in his own way. Whatever we may say about the sweetness and beauty of Mary, as we see her sitting in such peaceful attitude at the feet of her Lord, we must not forget that it was not Martha's service which Jesus reproved, but her anxious, fretful worry. Her service was important, was even essential to our Lord's own comfort, and to her true and hospitable entertainment of him in her home. The Marys are very lovely; and every woman should have the Mary-spirit of peace, and should sit much, Mary-like, at the Master's feet to hear his words, in order to be fitted for the best service. But Martha's work must be done too: no true Christian woman will neglect her duties of service in her privileges of devotion.

> "Yea, Lord. Yet some must serve.
>   Not all with tranquil heart,
> Even at thy dear feet,
> Wrapped in devotion sweet,
>   May sit apart.
>
> Yea, Lord. Yet some must bear
>   The burden of the day,
> Its labor and its heat,
> While others at thy feet
>   May muse and pray.
>
> Yea, Lord. Yet some must do
>   Life's daily task-work: some
> Who fain would sing, must toil
> Amid earth's dust and moil,
>   While lips are dumb.

> Yea, Lord. Yet man must earn,
>   And woman bake the bread;
> And some must watch and wake
> Early for others' sake,
>   Who pray instead.
>
> Yea, Lord. Yet even thou
>   Hast need of earthly care.
> I bring the bread and wine
> To thee, O Guest divine!
>   Be this my prayer."

Let each of these good women follow the Master closely, see as much as possible of the infinite loveliness of his character, and copy into her own life all she can see; yet let her not imagine that she has seen or copied all of Christ, but let her look at every other Christian woman's life with reverence, as bearing another little fragment of the same divine likeness. Let every man do earnestly and well the particular work which he is fitted and called to do, but let him not imagine that he is doing the only kind of work which God wants to have done in this world; rather let him look upon every faithful servant who does a different work as doing a part equally important and equally acceptable to the Master.

The bird praises God by singing; the flower pays *its* tribute in fragrant incense as its censer swings in the breeze; the tree shakes down fruits from its bending boughs; the stars pour out their silver beams to gladden the earth; the clouds give their blessing in gentle rain: yet all with equal faithfulness fulfil their mission. So among Christ's redeemed servants, one serves by incessant toil in the home, caring for a large family; another by silent example as a sufferer, patient and uncomplaining; another with the pen, sending forth words that inspire, help, cheer, and bless; another by the living voice, whose eloquence moves men, and starts impulses to better, grander living; another by the ministry of sweet song; another by sitting in quiet peace at Jesus' feet, drinking in his spirit, and then shining as a gentle and silent light, or pouring out the fragrance of love like a lowly and unconscious flower; yet each and all of these may be serving Christ acceptably, hearing at the close of each day the whispered word, "Well done."

CHAPTER V.

THY WILL, NOT MINE.

"Our lives we cut on a curious plan,
Shaping them, as it were, for man;
But God, with better art than we,
Shapes them for eternity."

MANY people only half read their Bibles. They skim the surface, and fail to get the full, deep meaning of the golden words. They get but half-truths, and half-truths ofttimes are misleading. Even inspired sentences standing alone do not always give the full and final word on the doctrine or the duty which they present: frequently it is necessary to bring other inspired sentences, and set them side by side with the first, in order to get the truth in its full, rounded completeness. When the Tempter quoted certain Scriptures to our Lord, he answered, "It is written again." The plausible word in its isolation was but a fragment, and other words must be brought to stand beside it to give it its true meaning.

Many mistaken conceptions of the doctrine of prayer come from this superficial reading of the Scriptures. One person finds the words, "Ask, and it shall be given you;" and, searching no farther, he concludes that he has a key for the unlocking of all God's storehouses; he can get any thing he wants. But he soon discovers that the answers do not come as he expected; and he becomes discouraged, and perhaps loses faith in prayer. The simple fact is, that this word of Christ standing alone does not contain the full truth about prayer. "It is written again." He must read more deeply, and, gathering all our Lord's sayings on this subject, combine them in one complete statement. There are conditions to this general promise. The word "ask" must be carefully defined by other Scriptures; and, when this is done, the statement stands true, infallible, and faithful.

One of the ofttimes forgotten conditions of all true and acceptable prayer is the final reference of every desire and importunity to the divine will. After all our faith, sincerity, and importunity, our requests must still be left to God, with confidence that he will do what is best. For how do we know that the thing we ask would really be a blessing to us if it came? Surely God knows better than we can know; and the only sure and safe thing to do is to express our desire with earnestness and faith, and then leave the matter in his hands. It is thus that we are taught, in all the Scriptures, to make our prayers to God.

But do we quite understand this? Is it not something far more profound than many of us think? It is not mere silent acquiescence after the request has been refused: such acquiescence may be stoical and obstinate, or it may be despairing and hopeless; and neither temper is the true one. To ask according to God's will is to have the confidence, when we make our prayer, that God will grant it unless in his wisdom he knows that refusal or some different answer than the one we seek will be better for us; in which case we pledge ourselves to take the refusal or the other answer as the right thing for us.

If we understood this, it would remove many of the perplexities which lie about the doctrine of prayer and its answer. We pray earnestly, and do not receive what we ask. In our bitter disappointment we say, "Has not God promised, that, if we ask, we shall receive?" Yes; but look a moment at the history of prayer. Jesus himself prayed that the cup of his agony —the betrayal, the trial, the ignominy, the crucifixion, and all that nameless and mysterious woe that lay back of these obvious pains and sorrows — might pass, and yet it did not pass. Paul prayed that the thorn in his flesh might be removed, yet it was not removed. All along the centuries, mothers have been agonizing in prayer over their dying children, crying to God that they might live; and even while they were praying, the shadow deepened over them, and the little hearts fluttered into the stillness of death. All through the Christian years, crushed souls, under heavy crosses of sorrow or shame, have been crying, "How long, O Lord! how long?" and the only answer has been a little more added to the burden, another thorn in the crown.

Are not our prayers answered, then, at all? Certainly they are. Not a word that goes faith-winged up to God fails to receive attention and answer. But ofttimes the answer that comes is not relief, but the spirit of acquiescence in God's will. The prayer many, many times only draws the trembling suppliant closer to God. The cup did not pass from the Master, but his will was brought into such perfect accord with the Father's, that his piteous cries for relief died away in a refrain of sweet, peaceful yielding. The thorn was not removed, but Paul was enabled to keep it and forget it in glad acquiescence in his Lord's refusal. The child did not recover, but the king was helped to rise, wash away his tears, and worship God.

We are not to think, then, that every burden we ask God to remove, he will surely remove, nor that every favor we crave, he will bestow. He has never promised this. "This is the confidence that we have in him, that, if we ask any thing according to his will, he heareth us." Into the very heart of the prayer which our Lord gave, saying, "After this manner pray ye," he put the petition, "Thy will be done." Listening at the garden-gate to the Master's own most earnest supplication, we hear, amid all the agonies of his wrestling, the words, "Nevertheless, not as I will, but as thou wilt."

The supreme wish in our praying should not, then, be merely to get the relief we desire. This would be to put our own will before God's, and to leave no place for his wisdom to decide what is best. We are to say, "This desire is very dear to me: I would like to have it granted; yet I cannot decide for myself, for I am not wise enough, and I put it into Thy hand. If it be Thy will, grant me my request: if not, graciously withhold it from me, and help me sweetly to acquiesce, for Thy way must be the best."

For example: your health is broken. It is right to pray for its restoration; but running all through your most earnest supplication, should be the songful, trustful, "Nevertheless, not as I will, but as thou wilt." You are a mother, and are struggling in prayer over a sick child. God will never blame you for the strength of your maternal affection, nor for the clasping, clinging love that holds your darling in your bosom and pleads to keep it. Love is right: mother-love is right, and, of all things on earth, is likest the love of God's own heart. Prayer is right, too, no matter how intense and importunate; yet, amid all your agony of desire, it should be the supreme, the ruling wish, subduing and softening all of nature's wild anguish, and bringing every thought and feeling into subjection, that God's will may be done.

> "Not as I will:" — the sound grows sweet
> Each time my lips the words repeat.
> "Not as I will:" — the darkness feels
> More safe than light, when this thought steals
> Like whispered voice to calm and bless
> All unrest and all loneliness.
> "Not as I will," because the One
> Who loved us first and best has gone
> Before us on the road, and still
> For us must all his love fulfil, —
>   "Not as we will."

The groundwork of this acquiescence is our confidence in the love and wisdom of God. He is our Father, with all a father's tender affection, and yet with infinite wisdom, so that he can neither err nor be unkind. He has a plan for us. He carries us in his heart and in his thought. The things we, in our ignorance, desire, might in the end work us great ill; the things from which we shrink may carry rich blessings for us; so we should not dare to choose for ourselves what our life experiences shall be. The best thing possible for us in this world is always what God wills for us. To have our own way rather than his, is to mar the beauty of his thought concerning us.

The highest attainment in prayer is this laying of all our requests at God's feet for his disposal. The highest reach of faith is loving, intelligent consecration of all our life to the will of God.

"Laid on thine altar, O my Lord divine!
Accept this gift to-day, for Jesus' sake.
I have no jewels to adorn thy shrine,
Nor any world-famed sacrifice to make:

But here I bring within my trembling hand
    This will of mine, — a thing that seemeth small;
And thou alone, O Lord! canst understand
    How, when I yield thee this, I yield mine all.

Hidden therein, thy searching gaze can see
    Struggles of passion, visions of delight,
All that I have or am or fain would be, —
    Deep loves, fond hopes, and longings infinite.
It hath been wet with tears, and dimmed with sighs,
    Clenched in my grasp till beauty it hath none:
Now from thy footstool, where it vanquished lies,
    The prayer ascendeth, ' May thy will be done.'

Take it, O Father! ere my courage fail,
    And merge it so in thine own will, that e'en
If in some desperate hour my cries prevail,
    And thou give back my gift, it may have been
So changed, so purified, so fair have grown,
    So one with thee, so filled with peace divine,
I may not know or feel it as mine own,
    But, gaining back my will, may find it thine."

When a beautiful life hangs trembling in the balance, we should not, with all our loving yearning, dare to choose whether it shall be spared to us, or carried home. When some great hope of our heart is about to be taken from us, we should not dare settle the question whether we shall lose it, or keep it. We do not know that it would be best. At least, we know that God has a perfect plan for our life, marked out by his infinite wisdom; and surely we should not say that what we, with our limited wisdom, might prefer, would be better than what he wants us to be.

CHAPTER VI.

GOD'S RESERVE OF GOODNESS.

God never gives all he has to give. The time never comes when he has nothing more to bestow. We never reach the best in divine blessings: there is always something better yet to come. Every door that opens into a treasury of love shows another door into another treasury beyond. The unrevealed is ever better than the revealed. We need not fear that we shall ever come to the end of God's goodness, or to any experience for which he will have no blessing ready.

Yet the divine goodness is not emptied out in heaps at our feet when we first start in faith's pathway; rather it is kept in reserve for us until we need it, and is then disbursed. The Scriptures speak of God's great goodness as *laid up* for them that fear him. This is the divine method, both in providence and in grace. We think of one gathering food in bright summer days, when the harvests are golden, when the fruits hang on bending boughs, when the hillsides are purple with their vintage, and laying up for winter's use, when the fields shall be bleak, and the trees and vines bare. Or we think of a father gathering riches, and securing them in safe deposits or investments for his children when they shall grow up. So God has laid up goodness for his people.

God laid up goodness in the creation and preparation of the earth. Ages before man was made, God was fitting up this globe to be his home, storing in mountain, hill, and plain, in water, air, and soil, and in all nature's treasuries, supplies for every human need. We think, for example, of the vast beds of coal laid up among earth's strata, ages and ages since, in order that our homes might be warmed and brightened in these later centuries; of the iron, silver, gold, and other metals secreted in the veins of the rocks; of the medicinal and healing virtues stored in leaf, root, fruit, bark, and mineral; and of all the latent forces and properties lodged in nature, to be called out from time to time to minister to human wants. No sane and sensible man will say that all this was accidental: it was divine forethought that laid up all this goodness for the welfare of God's children.

The same is true of spiritual provision. In the covenant of his love, in the infinite ages of the past, God laid up goodness for men. Redemption was no afterthought: it was planned before the foundation of the world. Then Christ, in his incarnation, obedience, sufferings, and death, laid up goodness for his people. We sometimes forget, while we pillow our heads on the promises of God, and rest secure in the atonement, and enjoy all the blessings of redemption and the hopes of glory, what these things cost our Redeemer. In those long years of poverty, those sharp days of temptation, those keen hours of agony, he was laying up treasures of blessing and glory for us. There is not a hope or a joy of our Christian faith that does not come to us out of the treasures stored away by our Redeemer during the years of his humiliation and the hours of his agony.

But all this goodness was *laid up*. The treasures were not all opened at the beginning. This is true, both in nature and in grace. So far as we know, there has been nothing new created since the beginning, but there has been a continual succession of developments of hidden treasures and powers to meet the new needs of the multiplying and advancing race. Thus, when fuel began to grow scarce, the vast coal-beds were discovered. They were not created then for the emergency: ages before, they had been "laid up," but the storehouse was only then opened to meet the world's want. So, when material for light was in danger of exhaustion, the reservoirs of oil, long hidden in reserve, were opened. And in these recent days, men are discovering the powers of electricity, — not a new creation, but an energy which has flowed silent and unperceived through all space from the beginning, only to become available in these later days. Human need is the key that unlocks the storehouses of God's provision for the children of men.

In spiritual things, the method is the same. Take the Bible for illustration. It is a great treasury of reserved blessing. There has not been a chapter, a line, a word, added to it since the pen of inspiration wrote the final Amen; yet every new generation finds new things in the Holy Book. This is true in all individual experience. As children we study the Bible, and con its words; but many of the precious sentences have no meaning for us. The light, the comfort, or the help is there, but we do not see it: indeed, we cannot see it until we have larger experience, and a fuller sense of need. For a time the rich truths of the Bible seem to hide away, refusing to disclose to us their meaning. We read them in sunny youth, but do not discover the blessing or help that is in them. Then we move on into the midst of the struggles, trials, and conflicts of real life, and new senses begin to reveal themselves in the familiar sentences. Promises that seemed pale before, as if written with invisible ink, begin to glow with rich meaning. Experience reveals their preciousness. Every Christian who has lived many years, and passed through trials and struggles, knows how texts with which he has been familiar from childhood, but in which he has never before found any special help, all at once, in some new experience of need or trial, flash out, like newly lighted lamps, and pour bright beams upon his path. The light was not new: it had shone there all the while; but he could not see it until now because other lights were shining about him, obscuring this one.

Most personal knowledge of the Bible has to be learned in this way. The words lie in our memory, and the years come and go, with their experiences. The light of human joy wanes; health gives way; disappointment comes; sorrow breaks in upon us; some human trust fails; the sunlight that flowed about us yesterday has gone out, and our path lies in darkness. Then the words of God that have lain so long in memory, without apparent brightness, flash out like heavenly lamps, and pour their welcome radiance all about us. Did those words have no light in them before? Yes: the lamps were shining all the while; but our eyes did not discern the brightness until this world's lamps went out, and it grew dark about us. The goodness was laid up, reserved until we needed it.

God's storehouses of spiritual truth never are opened to us until we really need their blessing. They are placed, so to speak, along our life-path, the right supply at the right point. By the plan of God, in every desert there are oases; at the foot of each sharp, steep hill, there are alpenstocks for climbing; in every dark gorge, there are lighted lamps; at every stream, there is a bridge. But we find none of these till we come to the place where we need them. And why should we? Will it not be soon enough to see the bridge when we stand by the stream? Will it not be soon enough, when it grows dark, for the lamps to shine out? Will it not be soon enough, when the larder is empty, for God to send bread?

The storehouse in which God's goodness is

laid up is found always at the point of need. Take a promise or two for illustration: "In the time of trouble, he shall hide me in his pavilion." It is very clear that we cannot get this promise when we are in joy and safety, but only when we are in peril. "When thou passeth through the waters, I will be with thee." This goodness is laid up in the midst of the wild waves, and cannot be found in any sunny field. "Leave thy fatherless children; I will preserve them alive: and let thy widows trust in me." This promise can never come to the tender wife when she leans on the strong arm of her husband, nor to the happy children when they cluster about the living, loving father's knee. It can be found only by the dark coffin or by the grave of love: it lies hidden amid the desolation of sorrow. Thus, the divine treasuries are placed in the midst of the very needs themselves, and we cannot get the help or the comfort until we stand within the circle of the need.

Many a mother, when she reads how some other Christian mother bore herself with sweet resignation when her child died, says, "I could not give up *my* child in that way: I have not grace enough to do it." But why should she have such grace now? It will be time enough when she needs it. *That* supply can be gotten at only when she is in the midst of the experience. While the child lives, the mother's duty is not sorrow, not submission, but rather, with loving fidelity, to train her child for this life, and for the life beyond; and for this duty, the mother will receive all needful grace, if she seeks it in faith. Then, if death comes to her child, grace will be given, enabling her to meet the bereavement, and sweetly to submit to God's disclosed will.

Many people dread death, and fear that they can never meet it with triumph; but God does not give grace for victorious dying when one's duty is to live. He gives then grace for living, grace for honesty, grace for fidelity, grace for heroism in life's battle: then, when death comes, when life's work is finished, and the hour comes for the departure, he will give dying grace. The storehouse in which *that* supply is laid up, is found only in the valley of shadows; and we cannot get the prepared and reserved goodness until we come to the experience to which it is pre-eminently suited.

The best of God's goodness is laid up in heaven : hence, to a Christian, death is always a glorious gain. A poet represents our first parent as trembling when he thought of the sun setting the first day of his life, and of night's coming. It seemed to him, that only calamity could result to this fair world. But, to his amazement, when the sun went down softly and silently, thousands of brilliant stars flashed out, and lo! creation infinitely widened in his view. The night revealed far more than it hid. Instead of fly, flower, and leaf, which the sun's beams showed, the darkness unveiled all the glorious orbs of the sky. So, similarly, we shun and dread death. It seems to be only darkness, and seems to hide the lovely things on which our eyes have looked; but, in reality, it will reveal far more than it hides. If it shuts our eyes to the little, perishing things of earth, it will unveil to us the splendors of eternity. The best things are laid up in heaven, and can only be gotten when we pass through death's gate into the Father's house.

Thus, this principle of reserved goodness runs through all God's economy. Blessings are laid up, and are given to us as we need them. Every experience brings to us its own store. Sorrow comes; but, veiled in the sorrow, the angel of comfort comes too. It grows dark, but then the lamps of promise shine out. Losses are met, but there is a divine secret that changes loss into gain. A bitter cup is given, but it proves to be medicine for our soul. Death comes, and seems the end of all: but, lo! it is only the beginning of life; for it leads us away from empty shadows to eternal realities.

CHAPTER VII.

THE BLESSING OF NOT GETTING.

"The good we hoped to gain has failed us. Well,
  We do not see the ending; and the boon
  May wait us down the ages,— who can tell?—
  And bless us amply soon.

In God's eternal plan, a month, a year,
  Is but an hour of some slow April day,
  Holding the germs of what we hope and fear
  To blossom far away."

THERE is one class of mercies and blessings of which we are not sufficiently ready to take note. These are the things that God keeps from us. We recount, with more or less gratitude, the good gifts that we receive from him; but there are many blessings that consist in our *not* receiving. In one of Miss Havergal's bright flashes of spiritual truth, she quotes these words of Moses to the Israelites: "As for thee, the Lord thy God hath not suffered thee so to do." Then she adds, "What a stepping-stone! We give thanks, often with a tearful, doubtful voice, for our spiritual mercies positive; but what an almost infinite field there is for mercies negative! We cannot even imagine all that God has suffered us *not* to do, *not* to be." There is no doubt that very many of the Lord's greatest kindnesses are shown in saving us from unseen and unsuspected perils, and in keeping from us things that we desire, but which would surely work us harm instead of blessing, were we to receive them.

There was a trifling accident to a railway-train one day, which caused an hour's delay. One lady on the train was greatly excited. The detention would cause her to miss the steamer, and her friends would be disappointed in the morning when she should fail to arrive. That night the steamer on which she so eagerly wished to embark was burned to the water's edge, and nearly all on board perished. Her feeling of grieved disappointment was changed to one of grateful praise to God for the strange deliverance he had wrought. A carriage drove rapidly to a station one afternoon, just as the train rolled away: it contained a gentleman and his family. They manifested much annoyance and impatience at the failure to be in time. Important engagements for to-morrow could not now be met. Sharp words were spoken to the coachman; for the fault was his, as he had been ten minutes late in appearing. An angry scowl was on the gentleman's face, as he drove homeward again. All the evening he was sullen and unhappy. In the next morning's papers he read an account of a terrible bridge accident on the railway. The train he had been so anxious to take, and so annoyed at missing, had carried many of its sleeping passengers to a horrible death. The feeling of bitter vexation and sullen anger was instantly changed to one of thanksgiving. In both these cases the goodness of God was shown in not suffering his children to do what they considered essential to their happiness or success.

These are typical illustrations. In almost every life there are similar deliverances at some time or other, though not always so remarkable or so apparent. There is no one who has carefully and thoughtfully observed the course of his own life, who cannot recall many instances in which providential interferences and disappointments have proved blessings in the end, saving him from calamity or loss, or bringing to him better things than those which they took out of his grasp. We make our plans with eager hope and expectation, setting our hearts on things which seem to us most radiant and worthy: then God steps in, and sets these plans of ours aside, substituting others of his own, which seem destructive. We submit, perhaps sullenly, with rebellious heart: it seems to us a sore adversity; but in a little while we learn that the strange interference, over which we struggled so painfully, and were so sorely perplexed, was one of God's loving thoughts, — his way of saving us from peril or loss. If he had let us have our own way, pain or sorrow would have been the inevitable result. He blessed us by not permitting us to do as we wished.

Who can tell from how many unseen and

unsuspected dangers he is every day delivered? When a passenger arrives at the end of a stormy voyage, he is thankful for rescue from peril; but when the voyage is quiet, without tempest or angry billow, he does not feel the same gratitude. Yet, why is not his preservation even more remarkable in this case than in that? He has been kept not only from danger imminent and apparent, but also from terror or anxiety. In an old-time gathering of clergymen, one of them asked the others to unite with him in thanksgiving to God for a signal deliverance on his way to the meeting. On the edge of a perilous precipice his horse had stumbled, and only the good hand of God had saved him from being hurled to death. Another clergyman asked that thanks might be given also for his still greater deliverance: he had come over the same dangerous road, and his horse had not even stumbled. Surely, he was right: he had still greater cause for thankfulness than the other. Each of our lives is one unbroken succession of such deliverances. There is not a moment when possible danger is not imminent. Yet we too often forget God's mercy in saving us from exposure to perils. We thank him for sparing us in the midst of life's accidents, but do not thank him for keeping us even from the alarm and shock of accident.

Passing into the realm of spiritual experiences, the field is equally large. God is continually blessing us by suffering us not to do certain things which we greatly desire to do. He thwarts our worldly ambitions, because to permit us to achieve them would be to suffer our souls to be lost or seriously harmed. One man desires worldly prosperity, but in his every effort in that direction he is defeated. He speaks of his failures as misfortunes, and wonders why it is that other men, less industrious and less conscientious, succeed so much better than he. He even intimates that God's ways are not equal. But, no doubt, the very disappointments over which he grieves are in reality the richest of blessings. God knows that the success of his plans would be fatal to the higher interests of his spiritual life. The best blessing God can bestow upon him is to suffer him not to prosper in his plan to gather riches, and to attain ease. The same is true of all other human ambitions. To let men have what they want, would be to open the gates of ruin and death for them. What they hunger for, thinking it bread, is but a cold stone. The path that to their eyes seems to be strewn with flowers, and to lead to a paradise, is full of thorns, and leads to darkness and death. The things they crave and cry for, thinking to find sweet satisfaction in them, when gotten at last prove to be but bitter ashes.

"I think God sometimes sends what we have cried for,
    Year after year in vain;
To prove to us how poor the things we've sighed for,
    And how beset with pain.
The human heart can know no greater trial
    Than comes with this confession,
That the continued sorrow of denial
    Was better than possession."

Sometimes the ways of God do seem hard. Our fondest hopes are crushed: our fairest joys fade like summer flowers. The desires of our hearts are withheld from us; yet, if we are God's children, we cannot doubt that in every one of these losses or denials a blessing is hidden. Right here we get a glimpse into the mystery of many unanswered prayers. The things we seek would not work us good in the end, but evil. The things we plead to have removed, are essential to our highest interests. Health is supposed to be better than sickness, but there comes a time when God's kindness will be most wisely shown by denying us health. He never takes pleasure in causing us to suffer; he is touched by our sorrows; every grief and pain of ours he feels. Yet he loves us too well to give us things that would harm us, or to spare us the trial that is needful for our spiritual good. It will be seen in the end, that many of the very richest blessings of all our lives have come to us through God's denials, his withholdings, or his shattering of our hopes and joys. When we are called to be Christians, we are not promised earthly ease and possession. True, we are told that we shall be heirs to a great legacy, — "heirs of

God, and joint heirs with Christ,"—but our legacy is not such as men in this world bequeath in their wills to their children. To be "joint heirs with Christ" implies that we must first share with him his life of self-denial and sacrifice before we can become partakers with him in the joys and glories of his exaltation.

> "My share! To-day men call it grief and death;
>   I see the joy and life to-morrow;
> I thank our Father with my every breath
>   For this sweet legacy of sorrow;
> And through my tears I call to each, 'Joint heir
> With Christ, make haste to ask him for thy share!'"

We should never forget that the object of all divine culture is to sanctify us, and make us vessels meet for the Master's use. To this high and glorious end, present pleasure and gratification must ofttimes be sacrificed. This is the true key to all the mysteries of Providence. Any thing that hinders entire consecration to Christ is working us harm; and though it be our tenderest joy, it had better be taken away. In one of Miss Havergal's poems she tells of one who had chosen the Master's service, but who could not yield the full measure that other lives could bring, because the Master had given her a charge to keep, —

> "A tiny hand, a darling hand, that traced
> On her heart's tablet words of golden love;
> And there was not much room for other lines."

Jesus wished her to do larger, wider work for him, to gather not one new gem, but many, for his crown.

> "And so He came:
> The Master came himself, and gently took
> The little hand in his, and gave it room
> Among the angel harpers. Jesus came,
> And laid his own hand on the quivering heart,
> And made it very still, that he might write
> Invisible words of power, — free to serve!
> Then through the darkness and the chill he sent
> A heat-ray of his love, developing
> The mystic writing, till it glowed and shone,
> And lit up all her life with radiance new, —
> The happy service of a yielded heart."

This is but one illustration of a discipline that is going on all the while in the lives of Christ's disciples. Prayer is not always granted, even when the heart clings with holiest affection to its most precious joy. Nothing must hinder our consecration. We should never think first of what will give us joy or comfort, but of what will work out God's holy will in us, and fit us for doing the service for him which he wants us to render. Pain is ofttimes better for us than pleasure, loss than gain, sorrow than joy, disaster than deliverance. Faith should know that God's withholdings from us when he does not give what we ask, are richer blessings than were he to open to us all the treasure-houses at whose doors we stand and knock with so great vehemence. Our unanswered prayers have just as real and as blessed answer as those which bring what we seek.

CHAPTER VIII.

"AFTERWARD."

> "Let us leave God alone!
> Why should I doubt he will explain in time
> What I feel now, but fail to find the words?"
>
> ROBERT BROWNING.

THERE is a wondrous power of explanation in "afterward." Things do not seem to us to-day as they will seem to-morrow. This is the key which the Scriptures give us for the solution of the strange mystery of affliction. "No chastening for the present seemeth to be joyous, but grievous; nevertheless, afterward it yieldeth the peaceable fruit of righteousness." There are many things in God's way with his people which, at the time, are dark and obscure, but which the future makes clear and plain. To-day's heavy clouds to-morrow are gone; and under the bright shining of the sun, and the deep blue of the sky, the flowers are sweeter, the grass is greener, and all life is more beautiful. To-day's tears to-morrow are turned to lenses through which eyes, dim no longer, see far into the clear heavens, and behold the kindliness and radiance of God's face.

One reason for the present obscurity of life is our ignorance, our limited knowledge. We know now only in part: we see only in a mirror darkly. We have learned merely the rudiments, and cannot understand the more advanced and abstruse things. A boy enters a school, and the teacher puts into his hand a Greek book, — a New Testament, we will say, — and asks him to read from the page before him; but he cannot make out a word of it; he does not know even the alphabet; it is a page of hieroglyphics to him. But the years roll on : he applies himself with diligence to the study of the language, and by patient degrees masters it. The day of his graduation comes, and the teacher again places in his hand the same page that puzzled and perplexed him on the day of his entrance. It is all plain to him now; he reads it with ease, and readily understands every word; he sees beauty in every line. Every sentence contains some golden truth. It is a page of St. John's Gospel: the words are those that fell from the lips of Christ himself, and are full of love, of wisdom, of heavenly instruction. As he reads them, they thrill his soul, and fill his heart with warmth and joy. Every line is bright now with the hidden fires of God's love. Riper knowledge has cleared away all the mystery, and unlocked the precious treasures.

We are all scholars in God's school. The book of providence is written in a language we do not yet understand; but the passing years, with their experiences, bring riper knowledge, and, as we learn more and more, the painful mysteries vanish. When we stand, at length, at the end of our school-days, the old, confusing pages will be plain and clear to us, as childhood's earliest lessons, though hard at the time, are afterward to ripe, manly wisdom. Then we shall see that every perplexed line held a golden lesson of wisdom for our hearts, and that the book of providence is but another of God's many testaments of love.

In one of George Macdonald's poems, a little child runs to her father, as he sits absorbed in his mental conflicts, and asks, "Father, what is poetry?" — "One of the most beautiful things that God has ever made," he replies. He opens a book, and shows her some poetry. She looks at it eagerly; but a shadow comes over her face, and she says, "I do not think that is so pretty." He then reads aloud some verses, and the reading pleases her; but still she cannot understand how poetry is beautiful. Her mother is beautiful, the flowers and the stars are beautiful; but poetry is not like any of these, and she cannot see the beauty in it. Then her father tells her she cannot understand until she is older, but that she will then find out for herself, and will love poetry well.

But the father's lesson was more for his own puzzled heart than for his child's. He, too, must wait until he had grown older and wiser, and then he would see the beauty he could not now see in God's strange providence.

We are all like little children. God writes in poetry which, no doubt, is very beautiful, as his eyes look upon it, and read its sentences; but we must wait to learn more before we can read the precious truths and golden thoughts which lie in the lines. In our sorrows and disappointments, good men come to us, and tell us that the Lord doeth all things well; that there is some blessing for us in every bitter cup; that the strange answers we get to our prayers are the very best things of God's love, though so disguised. We open the Bible, and we find there the same assurances; but we cannot see the blessing, the good, the love, in the painful and perplexing experiences of our lives. To our dim eyes, all is darkness, and our faith is well-nigh staggered. Then our Lord's word comes to us, "What I do, thou knowest not now; but thou shalt know hereafter. "Afterward" is the key. Possibly in this world, certainly in the great "hereafter" of heaven, we shall see that every providence of God, even the providences that were painful, and that seemed adverse, meant blessing and good. No doubt, we shall see, too, that many of the richest blessings of our lives, as they stand in radiant brightness before Christ's face, have come from the experiences that were most painful and most unwelcome.

> " This life is one; and in its warp and woof
> There runs a thread of gold that glitters fair,
> And sometimes in the pattern shows most sweet
> Where there are sombre colors."

Another reason why many of God's ways seem so strange to us, is because we see them only in their incompleteness. We must wait until they are finished before we can fully understand God's intention in them, or see the beauty that is in his thought. We stand by the sculptor's block when he is busy upon it with mallet and chisel, and to our eye it appears rough, with no lines of beauty; but we see it afterward, when it is unveiled to the world, and it seems almost to breathe, so perfect is the finished statue. A building is going up. There is now but an unsightly excavation, with piles of stones, timbers, and iron columns lying all about in confusion: afterward, however, we return, and a fine structure stands before our eyes, noble and majestic. Neither the statue nor the building was beautiful in its incompleteness. At present we see God's work in us and for us only in the process, not in its finished state: when it is complete, we shall understand why it was done in this way or in that.

> "As when some workers, toiling at a loom,
>   Having but little portions of the roll
>   Of some huge fabric, cannot see the whole,
>   And note but atoms, wherein they entomb —
>   As objects fade in evening's first gray gloom —
>   The large design, from which each trifling dole
>   But goes to make the long much-wished-for goal,
>   So do we seek to penetrate the doom
>   That lies so heavily upon our life,
>   And strive to learn the whole that there must be;
>   For each day has its own completed piece.
>   The whole awaits us, where no anxious strife
>   Can mar completeness: here but God's eyes see
>   What death shall show us when our life shall cease."

The marble might complain of the strokes, which seem only to cut it away, wasting its substance; but when the statue stands forth, the marvel and admiration of all eyes, it would complain no longer. The vine might cry out under the sharpness of the pruning-knife, as many of its finest branches are removed; but when it hangs laden with purple clusters, its cry of pain would become a song of joy.

> " Now, the pruning, sharp, unsparing,
> Scattered blossom, bleeding shoot;
> Afterward, the plenteous bearing
> Of the Master's pleasant fruit."

Most things look different when viewed from different points and in different lights. Events and experiences do not appear the same when we are in the midst of them, and after we have passed through and beyond them. The afterview, however, is the truest. This is especially so of life's sorrows: as we endure them, they are grievous; but afterward the fruits of peace appear. In the Canton of Bern, in the Swiss Oberland, a mountain stream rushes in a torrent toward the valley, as if it would carry destruction to the villages below; but, leaping from the sheer precipice of nearly nine hundred feet, it is caught in the clutch of the winds, and sifted down in fine, soft spray, whose benignant showering covers the fields with perpetual green. So sorrow comes, a dashing torrent, threatening to destroy us; but by the breath of God's Spirit it is changed as it falls, and pours its soft, gentle showers upon our hearts, bedewing our withering graces, and leaving rich blessings upon our whole life.

We should learn to trust God, even when the hour is darkest. The morning will surely come, and in its light the things that alarm us now will appear in friendly aspect; and in the forms we have dreaded so much, we shall see the benign face of Jesus as he comes to us in love. The ploughings of our hearts are but the preparation for fruitfulness. The black clouds that appear so portentous of evil pass by, leaving only gentle rain, which renews all the life, and changes desert to garden.

> "What shall thine 'afterward' be, O Lord?
>   I wonder, and wait to see
>   (While to thy chastening hand I bow)
>   What peaceable fruit may be ripening now,—
>   Ripening fast for me."

CHAPTER IX.

THE BLESSEDNESS OF LONGING.

"God loves to be longed for, he loves to be sought;
  For he sought us himself with such longing and love,
  He died for desire of us, marvellous thought!
  And he yearns for us now to be with him above."
                                                                    FABER.

AT first thought, a condition of longing would seem to be undesirable, and far from blessedness. Longing suggests unhappiness, discontent, the absence of that peace which seems to us to represent the loftiest state of blessedness, and the highest ideal of the life of faith. To have all our longings satisfied, we are apt to regard as the most desirable human condition. Yet, when we think more deeply of it, we know that there is a blessedness in longing. Our poet's words are true:—

"Of all the myriad moods of mind
  That through the soul come thronging,
Which one was e'er so dear, so kind,
  So beautiful as longing?"

If this appear too strong, we have to remember that one of our Lord's beatitudes was for those who long. "Blessed are they which do hunger and thirst after righteousness: for they shall be filled." Longing is, then, a healthful state; one that has an upward look, and has the promise of spiritual enriching. Satisfaction with one's attainments or achievements in any line, but especially in spiritual life and in personal holiness, is not an encouraging condition and may be unhealthful, even a mark of incipient decay.

Probably the most perfect piece of marble ever wrought by human hands is the statue of the Christ by Thorwaldsen. Those who have seen it in the Metropolitan Church at Copenhagen say that the whole light of the story of the gospel seems to stream down upon them from the stone as they look at it. The artist wrought a long while upon it, and with intense joy and enthusiasm; but when at last the statue was completed, a deep melancholy settled over him. When asked the reason for this, he said that his genius was decaying.

"Here is my statue of Christ: it is the first of my works with which I have ever felt satisfied. Till now my ideal has always been far beyond what I could execute, but it is no longer so: I shall never have a great idea again." To Thorwaldsen, satisfaction with his work was the sure indication of the limit of achievement. He felt that he would grow no more, because there was now no longing in his soul for any thing better.

In all life this law applies. In the physical realm, hunger is a mark of health, and the want of appetite proclaims disease. So the mind grows through longing. The doors of knowledge are opened to the student's eye, giving a glimpse of the boundless fields that stretch in all directions, and producing a craving, a hunger to know, which leads him to seek with eagerness for the rich treasures of wisdom. So long as this mind-hunger continues, the quest for knowledge will continue, and ever new stores will be discovered; but, whenever the hunger ceases, mental growth is at an end, and the mind has gained and passed its best achievements.

In spiritual life the same is true. There is no mood so hopeful as longing. The highest state is one of hunger and thirst, intense desire for more life, more holiness, more power, closer communion with God, more of the divine likeness in the soul. The gospel promises rest to those who come to Christ. Peace was one of the benedictions the Saviour left for his people. Contentment is one of the graces and duties enjoined upon the Christian, but spiritual hunger is not incompatible with either peace or contentment. It is not unrest; it is not anxiety or worry; it is not murmuring discontent: it is deep longing for more and ever more of all blessings, — calmer rest, sweeter peace, more perfect contentment, with richer heart-fulness of Christ, and more and more of all the gifts of the Spirit. It is depicted in the Psalms as an intense thirst for God, not the bitter cry of an unforgiven soul for mercy, but the deep, passionate yearning of a loving spirit for closer, fuller, richer, more satisfying communion with God himself. We find it in the life of the greatest of the apostles, who, wherever we see him, on whatever radiant height, is still pressing on, with unsatisfied longing and quenchless ardor, toward loftier summits and more radiant peaks, crying ever for more intimate knowledge of Christ, and more and more of the fulness of God. The ideal Christian life is one of insatiable thirst, never pausing in any arbor of spiritual content, but ever wooed on by visions of new joys and attainments.

The absence of this longing tells of the cessation of spiritual growth. Longing is the very soul of all true prayer. If we desire nothing more, we will ask nothing more. Longing is the empty hand reached out to receive new gifts from heaven; it is the heart's cry which God hears with acceptance, and answers with more and more; it is the ascending angel that climbs the starry ladder to return on the same radiant stairway with blessings from God's very throne; it is the key that unlocks new storehouses of divine goodness and enrichment; it is the bold navigator that ventures out on unknown seas, and discovers new continents; it is, indeed, nothing less than the very life of

God in the human soul, struggling to grow up in us into the fulness of the stature of Christ. Longing is the transfiguring spirit which purifies these dull, earthly lives of ours, and changes them little by little into the divine image.

> " The thing we long for, that we are
> For one transcendent moment; "

and continued longing after the good lifts us up into the good. The heavenly ideal ever kept before the mind, and longed after with intensity of desire, carves itself in the soul. As Lowell says again, —

> " Longing is God's fresh, heavenward will
> With our poor earthward striving :
> We quench it that we may be still
> Content with merely living.
> But, would we learn that heart's full scope
> Which we are hourly wronging,
> Our lives must climb from hope to hope,
> And realize our longing."

The latter half of this stanza must not be overlooked. If longing is God's angel to lead us heavenward, we must follow where the angel leads. Mere longing opens no gates, takes us to no heights, finds no rich treasures, discovers no new worlds. Longing without action is a most unhealthy state: it is but a poor sentimental day-dreaming, which leaves the soul more empty than ever when the dreams have vanished. Longing, to be blessed, must become an inspiration. When Raphael was asked how he painted such wonderful pictures, he said, "I dream dreams, and see visions; *and then I paint my dreams and my visions.*" With marvellous skill his hand wrought into forms of radiant beauty the lovely creations of his mind: otherwise they would never have brightened the world with their wondrous splendors. Longing not only sees the heavenly visions, but is obedient to them, and strives to realize them. It struggles up toward the excellence that shines before it: it seeks to attain the fine qualities which it admires. It is not satisfied with good resolves, but sets forward to make them come true. When Joan of Arc was asked what virtue she supposed dwelt in her white standard that made it so victorious, she replied, "I said to it, 'Go boldly among the English,' *and then I followed it myself.*" The white banner without "the lily-white maid" herself would have won no victories. So, when we send out the white banners of pure and noble longings, we must be sure to follow them ourselves, if we would win the blessings which our hearts crave.

> "I will not waste one breath of life in sighing;
> For other ends has life been given to me, —
> Duties and self-devotion, daily dying
> Into a higher, better life with Thee,
> My God, with Thee."

Every longing should at once become an active impulse in the soul. The hand should instantly be reached out to paint or carve the beauty of which the heart dreams, and for which it longs. Our longings should lead us into all paths of Christly service and all heroic duty. Mere gazing heavenward after the ascended Christ, and waiting and watching for his return, is not the way to realize the blessed glory. There is work to do to prepare for his coming, and he will come soonest and with greatest joy to those who do most to advance his kingdom.

CHAPTER X.

THE COST AND WORTH OF SYMPATHY.

> "If thou art blest,
> Then let the sunshine of thy gladness rest
> On the dark edge of each cloud that lies
> Black in thy brother's skies.
> If thou art sad,
> Still be thou in thy brother's gladness glad."
> HAMILTON.

THE true nature of sympathy is not always understood: it is more than tears, which often lie near the surface, and flow easily at the touch of any external experience. Some natures are wonderfully sensitive to the expressions of joy or sorrow in other lives. You stand before a cliff, and in responsive echo every sound that is made beside you comes back to your ear. If a child cries, the cliff sobs back. The murmur of a soft song returns again, like a melody sung by some far-away singer. The notes of speech come back echoing through the air. The cliff is sensitive to every wave of sound, and responds to it. There are human hearts that are similarly sensitive to every touch of human experience that plays upon them: they are so full of emotion, that they respond to every note of joy or sorrow that strikes their chords. They echo back the merry laughter, the voice of tenderness, the wail of sorrow, but they are nothing more than echoes: only from their surface do they reflects the tones of other lives. No depths are stirred. They know nothing of sympathy. Sympathy is more than an echo: its background is individual experience. Strength is not enough for this ministry of sympathy, even the purest, noblest, most majestic strength: it must have passed through the fires of suffering, or of struggle, to get the fineness and delicacy required for this sacred work. Moral uprightness and purity are not enough: unchastened, even these divine qualities are too cold to render the service that sad and weary hearts need in their loneliness and weakness. Even the purest holiness must be swept through by the thrills of pain before it can understand the experience of pain in others, and be made capable of feeling with them in their weakness and suffering. One may have pity without knowing any thing of the experience of the condition which appeals to him; but pity is not sympathy. Holy angels can pity the sons of men in their sore need, but in their lofty heights of unfallen purity they cannot sympathize with us mortals.

> " Not pity gazing from a height
>   In shining and immaculate light,
>   Can touch the sorrow-stricken soul,
>   And make it glow with warmth again;
>   But love — 'tis love can ease the pain,
>   'Tis love can make the heart feel whole."

Even Christ was not fitted to sympathize with men until he had entered into human flesh, and lived an actual human life. One would say that his divine omniscience certainly qualified him for sympathy. He knew already every phase of experience, — in the sense that his eye saw into every nook and cranny of every human heart, — and discerned and understood every play of emotion, every struggle, every pain; yet his omniscience did not prepare him for true sympathy: he must become a man. Nor was that enough: he might have taken humanity upon him, and then have passed at once with it into the glory of heaven. But he must live an actual human life; his nature must be enriched by experience; he must know life, not merely by his omniscience, but by having passed through it himself. This is the background of the precious doctrine of Christly sympathy. Christ was tempted in all points, and therefore he can be touched by the feeling of our infirmities. No matter what the phase of trial or struggle on which he looks down upon the earth, he can say, "I understand that. At Galilee, or at Bethany, or in the wilderness, or in Gethsemane, or on Calvary, I passed through that same phase of experience."

So even the tenderest human life — the one most responsive to external emotional influences — cannot truly sympathize with our lives until it has been enriched by experiences of its own. The young man brought up in a sequestered home, away from the mad excitements of the world, cannot understand, nor sympathize with, the struggles of the man who is wrestling with the sore temptations of a great city. The young woman who has never herself suffered, who has never had a wish ungratified nor a hope thwarted, nor has ever endured a pang or a grief, is not fitted to sit down beside a sister woman in sore agony over a shattered joy or a crushed hope, and really understand her feelings, or enter into actual sympathy with her.

Every one knows how fruit ripens. There are a thousand influences that play upon it all the summer through, — influences of climate, of sun and rain, of cold and heat, of darkness and light. Some fruits wait, too, for the frosts of autumn to come to complete the process of ripening. In some such way human life ripens. There are countless influences, — trial, joy, struggle, hardship, toil, ease, prosperity, adversity, success, failure, — and at last the character is mellow and gentle.

The old people understand this. Disappointments, bereavements, anxieties, tender joys, the deep ploughing of the heart by afflictions, and all the diversified experiences of threescore or fourscore years, — how they enrich the heart that is held all the while close to Christ under the warmth of his love! This is one of the blessed qualities of a ripe and beautiful Christian old age, that we sometimes overlook or underestimate. How much the aged know about life, if they have lived it well! What a power of helpfulness such an enriching puts into their hearts! No ministry in this world is finer than that of those who have learned life's secrets in the school of experience, and then go about, inspiring, strengthening, and guiding younger souls who come after them.

A heart thus disciplined is prepared for sympathy, in the deepest, truest sense. It needs no labored words of explanation to enable it to understand the stress and strain of trial, the bitterness of sorrow, or the burden of infirmity. It has felt the same, and now is thrilled by the experience on which it looks. Sympathy is a wonderful thing; it has a strange and mighty power of inspiration in it. How strong it makes us to go on with our work, to know that others care for us, and are interested in us! There is something in the simple touch of a friendly hand, or the look of a kindly eye, or the emotion that plays on an earnest face, that sends a quickening thrill through our souls. When one is in deep sorrow, how is he strengthened to bear it by feeling the pressure of a warm clasp, which tells him, better than any words could do, of sincere sympathy! It cannot bring back his dead; it cannot restore the shattered idol; it cannot calm the storm that is raging about him; it cannot remove a straw of the burden, nor eliminate one line of the chapter of grief: but there is another human heart close by that feels for him; there is a loving presence creeping up in the darkness close beside him; there is companionship; he is not alone, and this blessed consciousness makes him strong.

A little token of love sent into your sick-room from some gentle hand, when human presences are shut out, telling of a heart outside that thinks about you, what a messenger of gladness it is! No angel's visit could be more welcome or more comforting. There is a story of a prisoner who had received nothing but severity in his prison-life, and knew nothing of human tenderness. One day a kindly man visited him, and spoke brotherly words, manifesting a sincere and hearty interest in him. It was a new and strange experience; and, after the man had gone away, he said, "I can stay here now, for I know there is one man, at least, in the great world outside, who cares for me, and has an interest in me." And that consciousness cheered and brightened for many days the gloom of his lonely incarceration. Life is full of similar illustrations.

> " A clasp of hands will oft reveal
> A sympathy that makes us feel
> Ourselves again ; we lose our care :
> And in our heart's first glad rebound
> At tender sympathy new found,
> The world once more seems bright and fair."

If we would, then, be fitted for this blessed ministry, we must be content to learn in the school of experience. Even Christ learned by the things he suffered. Angels are not fitted for sympathy, for they know nothing about human life. In a picture by Domenichino, there is an angel standing by the empty cross, touching with his finger one of the sharp points in the thorn-crown which the Saviour had worn. On his face there is the strangest bewilderment. He is trying to make out the mystery of sorrow. He knows nothing of suffering, for he has never suffered. There is nothing in the angel nature or in the angel life to interpret struggle or pain. The same is measurably true of untried human life. If we would be sons of consolation, our natures must be enriched by experience. We are not naturally gentle to all men. There is a harshness in us that needs to be mellowed. Human uprightness undisciplined, is apt to be stern and severe, even uncharitable, toward weakness. We are apt to be heedless of the feelings of others, to forget how many hearts are sore, and carry heavy burdens. We have no sympathy with infirmity, because we do not know from experience what it means. We are not gentle toward sorrow, because our own hearts never have been ploughed. We give constant pain to sensitive spirits by word and act, because we have not learned that gentle delicacy and thoughtful tenderness which can be learned only through the careless wounding of our own feelings by others. These are lessons we can learn in no school but that of personal experience. The best universities cannot teach us the divine art of sympathy. We must walk in the deep valleys ourselves, and then we can be guides to other souls. We must feel the strain, and carry the burden, and endure the struggle, ourselves, and then we can be touched, and can give help to others in life's sore stress and poignant need.

"May I reach
That purest heaven, — be to other souls
The cup of strength in some great agony,
Enkindle generous ardor, feed pure love,
Beget the smiles that have no cruelty,
Be the sweet presence of a good diffused,
And in diffusion ever more intense!"

CHAPTER XI.

FINDING ONE'S MISSION.

"To do God's will, that's all
That need concern us; not to carp or ask
The meaning of it, but to ply our task,
Whatever may befall;
Accepting good or ill as he may send,
And wait until the end."

ONE of the most inspiring of truths is, that God has a distinct plan for each one of us in sending us into this world. Not only does he create us all to be useful, to take some part in the world's affairs, to honor and glorify him in some way, but he designs each person for some definite place and some specific work. He does not send us into life merely to fill any niche into which we may chance to be lifted by the vicissitudes of life, or to do whatever bits of work may drift to our hands in the vast and complicated mesh of human affairs. God has a great plan, embracing "all his creatures and all their actions;" and in this plan every intelligent being has an allotted place and an assigned part. God has, therefore, a distinct thought and purpose for each one of us; and a true life is one in which we simply fulfil the divine intention concerning us, occupy the place for which we were made, and do the particular work set down for us in God's plan.

A distinguished preacher has said, "There is a definite and proper end and issue for every man's existence, an end which to the heart of God is the good intended for him, or for which he was intended; that which he is privileged to become, called to become, ought to become; that which God will assist him to become, and which he cannot miss save by his own fault. Every human soul has a complete and perfect plan cherished for it in the heart of God, — a divine biography marked out, which it enters into life to live." Surely this is a great thought, and one that gives to life — to each and every life, the smallest, the obscurest — a sacred dignity and importance. Nothing can be trivial or common which the great God thinks about, plans, and creates. The lowliest place in this world, to the person whom God made to occupy that place, is a position of rank and honor glorious as an angel's seat, because it is one which God formed an immortal being in his own image, and with immeasurable possibilities, to fill. George MacDonald says, "I would rather be what God chose to make me than the most glorious creature that I could think of; for to have been thought about, born in God's thought, and then made by God, is the dearest, grandest, and most precious thing in all thinking."

The question of small or great has no place here. To have been thought about at all, and then fashioned by God's hands to fill any place, is glory enough for the grandest and most aspiring life. And the highest place to which any one can attain in life is that for which he was designed and made. The greatest thing any one can do in this world is what God made him to do, whether it be to rule a kingdom, to write a nation's songs, or to keep a little home clean and tidy. The true problem of life is not to "get on," or to "get up," as men phrase it, not to be great, or to do great things, but to be just what God meant us to be. If we fail in this, though we win a place far more conspicuous, our life is a failure.

An intensely practical question, therefore, is, How may we find our place,— the place for which God made us? How can we learn what he wants us to do in his great world, with its infinity of spheres and occupations? How may we be sure that we are fulfilling our part in God's great plan? In the olden days, men were sometimes guided to their missions by special revelation. In the absence of such supernatural direction, how may we know for what God made us?

It is very clear, for one thing, that we must put ourselves under God's specific guidance. We get this lesson from Christ's perfect life. He did only and always his Father's will. On his lips continually were words like these: "I must work the works of him that sent me:" "I came not to do mine own will, but the will of him that sent me." Even in the garden, in the hour of his bitterest agony, it was, "Nevertheless not my will, but thine, be done." Moment by moment he took his work from his Father's hand: he laid no plans of his own. He knew there was a definite part in the Father's great plan which belonged to him, and he wished only to do that. If we would find our mission, and fill our allotted place, and do the work assigned to us, we must do God's will, not our own. All our personal ambitions must be laid at his feet, all our plans submitted to him, either to be accepted, and wrought into his plan, or set aside for his better way. If we have truly given ourselves to God, we have nothing to say about the disposal of our lives: they are in his hands to do with as he pleases. If he interrupts us in our favorite pursuits, or breaks into our plans with some other work, or by laying us aside for a time, we should not chafe or fret. Our time belongs to him, and he knows what he wants us to do any day. If we are truly taking our life's direction from him, we must always be ready to forego our schemes and plans, and take instead whatever he allots. This is where the hardest battle has to be fought, for we are loath to give up our personal ambitions. When we have gotten thus far along, what remains is not so hard. One who is really ready to do God's will, and be just what God wants him to be, will surely in some way be led into his true place.

As for the direction itself, God gives it in many ways. The Bible is the basis of all right living. There we learn the divine will and our duty. No one can ever find his allotted place in God's plan who does not follow the divine commandments. There is no use asking about our mission, unless we are walking in the straight and clean paths marked out by the Holy Scriptures.

For specific guidance at points along the way, conscience, the voice of God in our own soul, must be listened for continually, and promptly and affectionately heeded. Providence also must be watched. God opens doors and closes doors. He brings us face to face with duties. He leads us up to opportunities. If we are ready to be guided, and have a clear eye for the handwriting of Providence, we shall not fail to be directed in the path on which God wants us to walk.

> "Blindfolded and alone I stand,
>   With unknown thresholds on each hand;
>   The darkness deepens as I grope,
>   Afraid to fear, afraid to hope:
>   Yet this one thing I learn to know
>   Each day more surely as I go,
>   That doors are opened, ways are made,
>   Burdens are lifted, or are laid,
>   By some great law, unseen and still,
>   Unfathomed purpose to fulfil,
>   'Not as I will.'"

People sometimes chafe because, in their circumstances, they cannot do any great things; as if nothing could be really a divine mission unless it is something conspicuous. A mother, occupied with the care of her little children, laments that she has no time nor leisure for any mission that God may have marked out for her. Does she not know that caring well for her children may be the grandest thing that could be found for her in all the range of possible duties? Certainly for her hands, for the time at least, there is nothing else in all the world so great. Organizing missionary meetings, speaking at conventions, attending Dorcas societies, writing books, painting pictures,— these are all fine things when they are the things God gives; but, if the mother neglects her children to do any of these, she has simply put out of her hands the largest things to take up those that are exceedingly small. In other words, that which the Master gives any one to do is always the grandest work he can find. The doing of God's will for any moment is ever the sublimest thing possible for that moment.

Another thing to be remembered in asking after one's mission, is that God does not usually map it all out at the beginning for any one. When the newly converted Saul accepted Christ as his life's Master, and asked what he should do, he got for answer, only that moment's duty. He was to arise, and go into the city; and there he would learn what to do next. That is the way the Lord generally shows men what their mission is, — just one step at a time, just one day's or one hour's work now, and then another and another as they go on. A young man at school grows anxious about what he shall be when he is through his course, what profession he shall choose, and frets and worries because he can get no light. He wonders why God does not make his duty plain to him; but what has the young man to do now with his profession or life-calling, when it must be years yet before he can enter upon it? His present duty is all he has to think of now; and that is simply to attend diligently and faithfully to his studies, to make the best possible use of his time and opportunities. One step at a time is the way God leads. One day's duty well done fits for the next.

A young school-girl is sorely perplexed over the problem of her life-duty: — ought she to go to a foreign-mission field, or devote herself to work at home? It will take her at least five years to complete the course of education on which she has just entered. Very clearly she has nothing to do, as yet, with the question which is causing her such perplexity. Her present duty is all that concerns her at the present time; and that is, to lay broad and strong foundations for a thorough education. What her ultimate mission in this world may be, God will show her in due time: about her mission just now, there need not be a moment's perplexity, for it is very plain. She has just to do well each day's routine of work, spending her time in diligent study. Common duties are the steps that lead upward and heavenward. God lights only one step of the path at a time; but, as we take that step, the light falls on another, and so on and on, thus lighting the whole path for our feet, until we are led at last to the gate that opens into heaven.

> "So live, so act, that every hour
> May die as dies the natural flower;
> That every word and every deed
> May bear within itself the seed
> Of future good in future need."

The way, therefore, to find out what God's plan is for our life, is to surrender ourselves to him in simple consecration, and then take up, hour by hour, the plain duties he brings to our hand. No matter about our mission as a whole: our only concern is with the moment we are now living, and the thing God wants us now to do. If each hour's work is faithfully done, we shall have at the last a whole life-work faithfully done. If we neglect the duties of the commonplace days while waiting for our mission, we shall simply throw our lives away, and utterly fail to fulfil the purpose of our creation.

> "No man is born into the world whose work
> Is not born with him; there is always work,
> And tool to work withal, for those who will:
> And blessèd are the horny hands of toil.
> The busy world shoves angrily aside
> The man who stands with arms akimbo set,
> Until occasion tells him what to do ;
> And he who waits to have his task marked out
> Shall die, and leave his errand unfulfilled."

CHAPTER XII.

LIVING UP TO OUR BEST INTENTIONS.

> " We hope, we aspire, we resolve, we trust,
>   When the morning calls to life and light;
>   But our hearts grow weary, and ere the night,
> Our lives are trailing in sordid dust.
>
> Wings for the angels, but feet for the men!
>   We must borrow the wings to find the way:
>   We may hope and aspire and resolve and pray,
> But our feet must rise, or we fall again."
>
> J. G. Holland.

If our best moods continually dominated our whole life, we should all live well. We all mean to live well: at least, there are times with all of us when we resolve to do so. New-Year's days, birthdays, communion Sundays, and other times, when the realities of life stand out in clearer relief than ordinarily, and impress us with unusual vividness, start in most of us serious thoughts, and inspire in us lofty aspirations and noble intentions. We are apt then to make excellent resolutions, and to start off in new and higher planes of living. Now, it would be well for us if there were some way of perpetuating these better moods, and living up to these good intentions. Too often, however, the serious impressions are but transient, and there is too little vitality in the good intentions and resolutions to make them really potent impulses for many days, or to give them permanence among the motives and forces of our life.

Of course, we cannot make our lives beautiful, merely by alternately adopting resolutions of amendment, and wailing out dolorous confessions of failure. Life runs deeper than words. Beauty is not fashioned by evanescent good intentions. Blemishes and stains are not covered up, nor are flaws mended, by penitential sighings of regret. Mere transient spasms of true living do not give grandeur to a life. If a temple is to be stable and stately, every stone from foundation to dome must be cut and set with care. If the texture of the fabric is to be beautiful and strong, every thread of web and woof must be bright and clean, and the weaving must be done with uniform skill and care. If a life is to be admirable when finished, its periodical good intentions must become strong, self-sustaining principles, shaping its every act, and ruling all its days and hours.

It ought not to be impossible to live up to the impulses of our best moods, or, at least, to do so to a much greater degree than most of us realize. In many of these good intentions, one element of weakness lies in their vagueness or indefiniteness. We simply resolve to be better this year than last, or to do more good in the future than in the past; but we have no clear and distinct conception in our minds of the points in which we will be better, or of the particular ways in which we will increase our usefulness. Our ideas of living better, and doing greater good, are nebulous and undefined.

We would be much more apt to succeed in our new purposes if we reduced them to definite and practical shape. In what respects will we amend our ways? This question starts another. What are our faults? Wherein do we fail in living? What are the mistakes we have been making? The answers to these questions will indicate to us the particular ways in which we need to live better. Then, in what definite ways shall we strive to be more useful? To what new Christian work shall we put our hands? Upon what new lines of service shall we enter? Just what old mistakes are we to avoid? If we would bring our vague, hazy ideas of greater usefulness down into some practical forms, and then enter at once upon the execution of our resolutions, they would be much more likely to become permanent, and to grow into our life.

There are many people who sigh over their poor Christian living and their far-awayness from Christ, and pray much, and earnestly too, for more faith, more love, greater nearness to the Saviour, who, after all, have no well-defined conceptions of the better things they would like to attain. Their sighings are little more than a vague and indolent discontent. They think they are sincere; but they are not, for they really do not want to be any better, or to have more of Christ, or do more in his service; if they did, they would soon be out of their poor, unsatisfactory condition. Truly earnest longings heavenward have a wondrous lifting power. There is a great deal of only imagined spiritual aspiration. Very much of our singing, "Nearer, my God, to Thee," is only the weakest kind of religious sentimentalism. Such vapid good intentions come to nothing, because there really are no good intentions to begin with. When the spiritual day-dreaming gets vigor enough to be worthy the name of desire or purpose, the higher attainments longed for will soon be reached. We must want what we ask in prayer, or we shall never get it. Then we must help to answer our own prayers, by reaching after, and struggling toward, what we want, and by climbing the steep paths that lead to the radiant heights.

Another element of weakness in many of our desires for better life and larger usefulness is, that we think of great and perhaps impossible attainments, and overlook the simple things that lie within our reach. No violent, overstrained exertions are necessary to a noble life, no superhuman efforts and achievements, — nothing but every-day duty faithfully done. The most of us must be content to live what are regarded as commonplace lives, without attracting the attention of the world, or winning the laurels of fame. We must, for the greater part, devote ourselves to the duties that spring out of our ordinary business, social, and domestic relations. The pressure of life's necessities is so great, that we cannot often turn aside to do things that lie outside of our common calling. Whatever service we render to Christ, must be rendered in and along the line of these relations, and while we are busied in the imperative duties which every day brings to our hands.

It is just at this point that many fail. They spend all their life seeking for the place in this world which they were intended to fill: they never settle down to any thing with any sort of restful or contented feeling. They have a lofty, though possibly a very nebulous, ideal of a wondrously brilliant life, to which they would like to attain, in which their powers would find full and adequate scope, and where they could achieve great things; but in their present condition, with its limitations, they can accomplish nothing worthy of their powers. So they go on discontented with their lot, and sighing for another; and, while they sigh, the years glide away; and soon they will come to the end, to find that they have missed every opportunity of doing any thing worthy of an immortal being in the passage from time to eternity.

The truth is, one's vocation is never some far-off possibility: it is always for the present the simple round of duties that the passing hour brings. Some one has pictured the days as coming to us with their faces veiled; but, when they have passed beyond our recall, the draped figures become radiant, and the gifts we rejected are seen to be treasures fit for king's houses. No day is commonplace, if only we had eyes to see the veiled splendors that lie in its opportunities, and in its plain and dull routine. There is no duty that comes to our hand but brings to us the possibility of kingly service, with divine reward.

We greatly mistake, therefore, if we think there is no opportunity for ordinary people to make their years radiant and beautiful by simply filling them with acceptable Christian service. There is room in the commonest relations of life, not only for fidelity, but for heroism. No ministry is more pleasing to the Master than that of cheery and hearty faithfulness to lowly duty, when there is no pen to write its history, nor any voice to proclaim its praise. To be a good husband — loving, tender, unselfish, and cherishing — or a good wife, — thoughtful, helpful, uncomplaining, and inspiring, — is most acceptable service. To live well in one's place in the world, adorning one's calling, however lowly, doing one's most prosaic work diligently and honestly, and dwelling in love and unselfishness with all men, is to live grandly. To fight well the battle with one's own lusts and tempers, and to be victorious in the midst of the countless temptations and provocations of every-day experience, is to be a Christian hero.

There is a field, therefore, for better living very close at home. It is in these common things that most of us must make our progress, and win our distinction, or fail, and be defeated. And there is room enough in these prosaic duties and opportunities for very noble and beautiful lives. There is nothing possible to a human soul nobler or greater than simple faithfulness. "She hath done what she could," was the highest commendation that ever fell from the Master's lips. An angel could do no more. When we are resolving to live more grandly in the future than in the past, it will help us to bring our eyes down from the far-off mountain-peaks, and from among the stars, where there is nothing whatever for us to do, and to look close about our feet, where lie many neglected duties, many unimproved opportunities, and many possibilities of higher attainment in spirit, in temper, in speech, in heart.

Another element of weakness in much of our resolving, is that we try to grasp too much of life at one time. We think of it as a whole, instead of taking the days one by one. Life is a mosaic, and each tiny piece must be cut with skill. The only way to make a perfect chain is to fashion each separate link with skill and care as it passes through our hands. The only way to make a radiant day is to make its each and every hour bright with the lustre of approved fidelity. The only way to have a year at its close stainless and beautiful, is to keep the days, as they pass, all pure and lovely with the loveliness of holy, useful living. It is thus, in little days, that our years come to us, and we have but the one small fragment to fill and beautify at a time. The year is a book, and for each day one fair white page is opened before us; and we are artists, whose duty it is to put something beautiful on the page; or we are poets, and are to write some lovely thought, some radiant sentence, on each leaf as it lies open before us; or we are historians, and must give to the page some record of work or duty or victory to enshrine and carry away.

It ought not to be hard to live well one day. Any one should be able to remember God, and keep his heart open toward heaven, and to remember others in need and suffering about him, and keep his hand stretched out in helpfulness, for just one day. Yet that is all there is to do. We never have more than one day to live. We have no to-morrows. God never gives us years, or even weeks: he gives us only days. If we live each day well, all our life will, in the end, be radiant and beautiful.

CHAPTER XIII.

LIFE'S DOUBLE MINISTRY.

A TWOFOLD influence attends and follows every life: the one is planned and intentional, the other is unpurposed and unconscious. A man lives fifty years of active life in a community, growing from poverty to wealth; and there are two classes of results left behind him when he is gone. There are the buildings he has erected, the business he has established and organized, the improvements he has made in the town, and the wealth he has accumulated: these are all purposed results. He lived to do these things; he thought about them, and then with labor and pains wrought them out; but while he has been toiling and building, with earnest ambition and intense energy, he has, day by day, been leaving behind him another class of results, which were not in his plans, and the columns of which he does not foot up when he estimates how much he has made during his life, or which he does not bequeath when he writes his will. These are the things he has done along the years of his busy life, by the words he has spoken in daily intercourse with men, by his manners and his dispositions, by the little wayside ministries which he has wrought ofttimes without conscious thought or intention, and through the silent influence that has flowed forth from his character and example, as fragrance is poured out on the air by a sweet flower, or as the soft beams of light stream in welcome radiance from a star.

Every life has this double history, and leaves this double record. In the ordinary reckoning of the results achieved by men, the purposed things only are counted. We say he made a million dollars; or we point to the bridges he built, or the cathedrals he planned, or the pictures he painted, or the books he wrote; or we say he travelled so many miles, and preached so many sermons, and made so many visits; or we sum up in our funeral eulogium the great and conspicuous things of his career, — and we think we have given all his biography; but we have not. There is a part of his history that is never written, that cannot be written; and it is probable that in nearly every life this is the better part, that a good man's unconscious, unrecorded, unintended influence aggregates more in the end than his purposed acts.

Any one who carefully notes the comparative value of lives in a community, will soon learn that the element which counts for the most, is that subtile thing which we call personal influence. One may give much money to religious and charitable objects; another may be an eloquent talker, and his voice may often be heard in public meetings; another may be enterprising, foremost in all progressive movements; another may be scholarly, a writer, an author, an oracle on all questions of learning; another may represent the best things in art, in taste, in whatever is beautiful and refined, — yet not one of these may impress himself on the community as does some quiet man, without either wealth or eloquence, or public spirit or scholarship, but who possesses that mysterious, indescribable power,

— a beneficent personal influence. There is something in him more subtile than money or speech, or activity or beauty, — a spiritual force, which flows out from his life, and touches all other lives, and strangely affects them. It is to him what fragrance is to a flower, what light is to a lamp: it is part of himself, and yet it reaches outside and beyond himself.

It is, so to speak, the projection of the man's own character, the flowing-out of his own life into other lives; it is the energy of the man's spirit working, as it were, beyond his body, and working without hands. In the good man, it is goodness, — goodness dwelling in his soul, and pouring out like light from the windows of a cottage on a dark night. In the Christian, there is more than mere human goodness: God's Spirit dwells in him. Every true Christian is in a sense a new incarnation. St. Paul said, "Christ liveth in me;" and he prayed for others that they might be "filled with all the fulness of God." The lamp that burns in a Christian's heart is the flame of the Divine Spirit, and the personal influence of a Christian becomes spiritual power. It is like the shadow of Peter: it has a healing, life-giving effect wherever it falls. Such a man goes about his daily duty as other men do; but while he is engaged in common things, he is continually dropping seeds of blessing, which spring up behind him in heavenly beauty and fragrance.

Every good life is constantly scattering these unconscious, unpurposed influences. A mother works hard all day in her home, keeping her house in order, preparing comforts for her family, watching over her children. She can tell, in the evening, just how many garments she has mended, how many rooms she has swept, and the entire day's history; but all day long she was patient, gentle, kind. At every turn, she had a bright smile for her children; she had cheering words and fond attentions for her husband; she had a pleasant welcome for the friends who called: in all these things she was unconsciously scattering seeds that will spring up in sweet flowers in other hearts and lives.

Who doubts which of these two ministries is in reality the richer and the more effective?

Yet the tired woman does not think of counting these wayside influences and services at all in her retrospect of the day's work. If she could do so, it would greatly cheer her, and strengthen her for a new day's life when it begins. She ofttimes comes to the day's close discouraged and depressed, because she has seemed to do so little beyond the endless routine of her household duties. When she sits down with her Bible, after all are quiet in her household, and looks back, she can scarcely recall one earnest word she has spoken for her Master. The whole day has been filled with earthly commonplace, and she thinks of it with pain and disheartenment; yet if she has lived sweetly and patiently amid her toils and worries, dropping cheerful words in the ears of her household, singing bits of song as she went about her work, bearing herself with love and faith amid all the experiences of the day, she has unconsciously performed a ministry of blessing, whose value she can never know till she gets to heaven.

A bit of written biography fits in here. A

young man, away from home, slept in the same room with another young man, a stranger. Before retiring for the night, he knelt down, as was his wont, and silently prayed. His companion had long resisted the grace of God; but this noble example aroused him, and was the means of his awakening. In old age he testified, after a life of rare usefulness, "Nearly half a century has rolled away, with all its multitudinous events, since then; but that little chamber, that humble couch, that silent, praying youth, are still present to my imagination, and will never be forgotten amid the splendors of heaven, and through the ages of eternity." It was but a simple act of common faithfulness, unostentatious, and without thought or purpose of doing good, save as the prayer would bless his own soul; yet there went out from it an unconscious influence, which gave to the world a ministry of rare power and value.

We do not realize the importance of this unconscious part of our life-ministry. It goes on continually. In every greeting we give to another on the street, in every moment's conversation, in every letter we write, in every contact with other lives, there is a subtle influence that goes from us that often reaches farther, and leaves a deeper impression, than the things themselves that we are doing at the time. After all, it is life itself, sanctified life, that is God's holiest and most effective ministry in this world, — pure, sweet, patient, earnest, unselfish, loving life. It is not so much what we *do* in this world, as what we *are*, that tells in spiritual results and impressions. A good life is like a flower, which, though it neither toil nor spin, yet ever pours out a rich perfume, and thus performs a holy ministry.

There is no place where this unconscious ministry is so potent as in the home. The lessons which parents teach their children are not one-thousandth part so important as the life they live before them day after day. This incident has appeared in some of the newspapers, and, though so homely, has its illustrative value: A gentleman who has a golden-haired little daughter, three years of age, took her to church for the first time the other day. At home she causes much amusement by attempts in cunning baby-fashion to do just as her father does. It was an Episcopal church, and she sat through the service and sermon with mature gravity and sedateness. It happened to be communion Sunday; and, being a communicant, her father went with others toward the chancel, unconscious that his little daughter was following him. As he knelt, and bowed his head, she took her place beside him, and bowed her head upon her tiny hands. The story is an example of what is going on perpetually in every home. The child is not merely imitating the parents' acts, but is drinking in their spirit, as flowers drink in the morning dew and the sunshine, to reproduce the same in permanent dispositions, tempers, and principles.

How, then, can we give direction and character to this unconscious ministry of our lives? When we do things voluntarily and with purpose, we can give shape to the effects; but how can we guard this perpetual outgoing of unintended influence? Only by looking well to our hearts. It is what we are when we are not posing before men, that we are really; and it is this which counts in this subtile ministry. We must *be*, therefore, in our own inner, secret lives what we want our permanent influence to be. This we can become, only by seeking more and more the permeation of our whole being by the loving, indwelling Spirit of Christ.

No one will say that this chance and undesigned ministry of good lives is not under God's direction. Though it is not in our thought to scatter the blessings which we thus unconsciously give out, it is certainly in his thought. Every influence of our lives, God uses as he will, to do good to whomsoever it pleases him to send the blessing.

> " Call you this chance ? A tiny seed
> Is blown by wandering winds that speed
> O'er land and sea. On ocean's breast
> 'Tis swept and whirled, then flung to rest
> Upon a lonely isle, 'mid reed
> And sedge, and many a straggling weed.
> Lo ! soon the isle a flowery mead
> Becomes, with brilliant blossoms drest.
> Call you this chance ?

> Ofttimes a word or kindly deed
> Bestowed upon some soul in need, —
> Some soul where Love is never guest, —
> Transforms the heart by hate opprest,
> Till flowers the noisome weeds succeed.
>   Call you this chance?"

Part of our every morning prayer should be, that God would use our influence for himself, and take the smallest fragments of power for good that drop from our lives, and employ them all for his glory, and as seeds to grow into beauty in some of this world's desert spots.

CHAPTER XIV.

THE MINISTRY OF WELL-WISHING.

> "It is not the deed that we do,
> Though the deed be never so fair,
> But the love that the dear Lord looketh for,
> Hidden with holy care,
> In the heart of the deed so fair."

THERE are few hearts in which there do not lie kindly wishes for others. The man must be depraved indeed who has only malign thoughts and desires for his fellow-men. Every Christian at least wishes others well, since love is the law of the regenerated life. There are occasions, too, when the good wishes find their way to the lips in kindly words. We say "Good-morning" when we meet a neighbor, and "Good-by" when we part from him. When our friends' birthdays come, we are in the habit of finding many delicate and pleasant ways of expressing our good will. The Christmas-time and the New-Year usually thaw out of our hearts the laggard good feelings, prompting us to many acts and words of kindness. It is well that our hearts have their seasons of generous blossoming, even if they are so brief, and are fixed by the almanac. It is well that any thing whatsoever has power to touch our lips with fire from the altar of love, and teach us to speak the gentle words which the lives about us are so hungry to hear.

One of the saddest things about life is, that, with such boundless power to give cheer to others by our speech, most of us pass through the world in silence, locking up in our own hearts the thoughtful and helpful words which we might speak, and which, if spoken, would minister so much strength and inspiration. Hearts are breaking with sorrow; men are bowing under burdens too heavy for them; duty is too large, battles are too sore. On every hand, and in every life, there is need for love's ministry, that men and women may not fail. Nor is it large and costly service that usually is needed: the kindly utterance of a kindly feeling will often give all the impulse and inspiration required. And the feeling is always close at hand, wanting but to be put into honest words, and spoken where the struggle is going on. Yet many of us let the good will lie in our heart unuttered, and stand by in silence while our brother beside us goes down in defeat which one word of ours would have changed into victory. It is not the want of love that is our fault, but the penuriousness which locks up the love, and will not give it out to bless others. Is any miserliness so mean? We let hearts starve to death close beside us, when in our hands is the food to keep them living, and make them strong: then when they lie in the dust of defeat, we come with our love to make funeral-wreaths for them, and speak eloquent eulogiums to their memory.

"What silences we keep year after year,
  With those who are most near to us and dear;
  We live beside each other day by day,
  And speak of myriad things, but seldom say
  The full, sweet word that lies just in our reach,
  Beneath the commonplace of common speech.

> Then out of sight and out of reach they go, —
> These close, familiar friends who loved us so;
> And sitting in the shadow they have left,
> Alone, with loneliness, and sore bereft,
> We think with vain regret of some kind word
> That once we might have said, and they have heard."

How much better it would be if, at all times, we gave freer rein to our lips in speaking kindly and cheering words! It is truly very sad when nothing less than the death of our friends can draw from our slow and selfish hearts the debt of love and of helpfulness that we owe them.

> "This is the cruel cross of life, to be
> Full-visioned only when the ministry
> Of death has been fulfilled, and in the place
> Of some dear presence is but empty space."

The warmest utterances then of love's good will cannot stir again the heart's chilled currents. It is too late to cheer the defeated spirit to new and victorious struggle. There is a time for the angel ministry: it is when the conflict is waging. When death has come, or failure or defeat, the opportunity is past forever.

The good wishes of friends do not, by their mere utterance, become realities in our lives: if they did, how rich most of us would be, and how happy! Good wishes, however, may be made to come true: they may be turned into prayers by those who make them, and, passing through the hands of Christ, may be changed from mere empty breath into blessings that shall enrich our lives, or feed our souls, or shine like sparkling gems upon our brows. The best way for our friends to get good things to us, is to pass them through Christ's hands.

No doubt, many of the good wishes that fall from the lips of those we meet are but empty forms, thoughtlessly uttered, with neither real desire nor fervor in the heart. Many of them, also, that are sincere enough, are wishes for very empty things. Happiness is the word into which so often the wish is coined, yet mere happiness is not by any means life's best blessing: it is but the ripple of laughter on life's surface. One may be happy, and never have one deep thought of life. Happiness is the product of merely earthly blessings, — friends, honors, pleasures, gold, — and these are the cheapest, and least valuable, and least satisfying things life can give. Wise and thoughtful friends will wish better things for us, — things that we can keep, things that will live on in us through all life's changes, and last over into the eternal years.

"Oh, the rare things which can never be brought
  From far-away countries, but still must be sought
  Through working and waiting, and anguish of thought!

The patience that comes to the heart, as it tries
To hear, through all discord and turbulent cries,
The songs of the armies that march to the skies;

The courage that fails not, nor loses its breath
In stress of the battle, but smilingly saith,
'I'll measure my strength with disaster and death;'

The love that through doubting and pain will increase;
The longing and restlessness, calmed into peace
That is perfect and satisfied, never to cease, —

These, these are the dear things! No king on his throne
Can buy them away from the poor and unknown
Who make them, through labor or anguish, their own."

It is in such qualities as these that we should seek to grow. Happiness is but like the sparkling dew that shines on the leaves and grasses in the summer morning, but is gone as soon as the sun's heat touches it. Life itself is deeper than happiness, and true blessings are those that are carved in life's own fibre. The good wishes that are of most worth are those that are for qualities of character, which we can carry with us through the pearl gate. The friends who think only of this world's beauties and honors and possessions and attainments when they wish us well, do not understand the table of values by which heaven estimates every thing.

How to get these great things into our lives is the question. Our best and truest friends cannot put them into our lives by any power of love: they may utter the wishes, and may translate them into prayers, but only we ourselves can take the benedictions and the answered prayers into our life. This we cannot do by mere resolving and purposing. New-Year or birthday resolutions are good enough as such; but unless they are gotten into the heart and life, as well as down in neat lines on paper, they will amount to little. Intentions may be very fine, but they must be lived out to become of practical worth. Rainbows are splendid pictures as they arch over the meadows and fields, but they vanish while you gaze at them: no hand is alert enough to grasp them, and hold them down upon earth. It is so with the lovely visions of excellence or of beauty that glow before us in our better moments: unless we set ourselves at once to work them into life, they will vanish into air. We must get our rainbows down out of the skies, and into our hearts. We must take the good wishes of our friends, and turn them into life: we must let them into our spirits, as the bare, briery rod in the garden lets the sunshine and the rain into itself, and transmutes them into blooming, fragrant roses.

Just how to do this, is an important question. The Bible emphasizes the fact that all growth of character must begin within. We are to be transformed by the renewing of our minds. Our hearts make our lives. What we are in heart, in spirit, in the inner life, we are really before God; and that, too, we shall ultimately become in actual character, in outward feature. The disposition makes the face. Every creature builds its own house to live in, and builds it just like itself. Coarseness builds coarsely: taste builds tastefully. A corrupt heart works through in the end, and changes all without into moral decay like itself. Jealousy, envy, bitterness, selfishness, all write their own image and signature on the features, if you give them time enough. A pure, beautiful soul builds a holy and divine dwelling for itself. In one of Goethe's tales, he tells of a wonderful lamp which was placed in a fisherman's hut, and changed it all to silver. The lamp of Christ's love, set in a human heart, transforms the life from sinfulness and earthliness into the likeness of Christ's own Spirit. To make good wishes come true, we must first get them into our heart, and then they will soon become real in our life.

No wish is more commonly expressed than that we may be happy, but true happiness depends altogether on the heart. A heart at peace fills our world with peace. Light shining in the bosom gives us light wherever we may be. The miners carry little lamps on their caps; and, wherever they move in the dark mines, there is light. So it is with us, if in us the lamp of joy shines. The world may grow very dark sometimes, but round about us there is always light. We shall surely be happy in the truest sense, if we have Christ's joy in our hearts. This is a lamp that shines through the longest night: no storm blows it out; indeed, its beams grow brighter the denser the gloom about us, and the fiercer the storm. Christ's joy was, in his own life, a lamp which was not quenched, even by the awful darkness of the cross.

If we would realize the wishes of our friends for joy, we must be sure to get the love of

Christ into our hearts, and then we shall always have our own lamp, and shall find gladness wherever we go. We need not, then, in any case greatly worry about our circumstances: if we are right within, all will be well. If the lamp is kept burning within the chamber, it will be light there, however deep the gloom outside.

CHAPTER XV.

HELPING WITHOUT MONEY.

> "'Tis a little thing
> To give a cup of water, yet its draught
> Of cool refreshment, drained by fevered lips,
> May give a shock of pleasure to the frame,
> More exquisite than when nectarean juice
> Renews the life of joy in happiest hours.
> It is a little thing to speak a phrase
> Of common comfort, which by daily use
> Has almost lost its sense; yet on the ear
> Of him who thought to die unmourned,
> 'Twill fall like choicest music."   TALFOURD.

THERE are not a few good people, with benevolent hearts and kindly impulses, who think they cannot do much good in the world because they have no money to give. They envy those who have wealth at their disposal, and who can so easily lift off the burdens of the poor, and give substantial aid to those who are in distress. They lament, that, because of their own poverty, they cannot relieve the human needs which they see about them. They do not know of any way of doing good without money, and sit discouraged in the midst of human needs and sorrows, not supposing that they with their empty hands could render any help or comfort.

No doubt, there are necessities which money only can relieve. Love, however rich and true and tender, will not pay the widow's rent, nor buy medicines for the sick man, nor put shoes on the orphan's feet. There always will be need for almsgiving while sin and sorrow continue on the earth, and he who has money to give must give it. "Whoso hath the world's goods, and beholdeth his brother in need, and shutteth up his compassion from him, how doth the love of God abide in him?" Our professed love for Christ will, if real, exhibit itself in love to his friends who are in need. We cannot now serve Christ in person with our acts and ministries, for he does not need what we can give; but his people are with us, and what we do for them we do for him. One of the old Christmas legends illustrates this truth.

Among the Saxons the custom prevailed of burning the Yule-log at the Christmas-tide. "A selfish man, who had plenty of money but no sympathy, was keeping his Christmas all alone; and out of deference to the day, he kept a little log burning with a very feeble flame. As he shivered in the chilly atmosphere of his desolate room, he fell asleep and dreamed. In his dream he heard a voice which drew his attention to a beautiful child who stood near him, and said, 'Jesus is cold.' With an impatient movement, the selfish man stirred the fire a little, and said, 'Why don't you go to the farmhouse down the lane? You'll be warm enough there.'—'Yes,' replied the child; 'but you make me cold, you are so cold.'—'Then, what can I do for you?'—'You can give me a gold coin.' With a great deal of reluctance, the money-chest was opened, and a gold coin was given to the child. He took it. Instantly the dingy room became bright and cheerful, as the child hung up some laurel and holly, saying, 'These are for life;' and placed two candles on the shelf, saying, 'These are for light;' and stirred the fire, saying, 'That is for love.' Then the door was thrown open, and a poor widow and a sick man, and orphan children, were brought in and seated at a bountiful repast, while the child kept saying, 'Jesus is warm now;' and the selfish man found that he also was enjoying the scene, so that he presently confessed, 'I think that I am warmer too.' Then the child suddenly disappeared, and in his place there was a divine presence; and solemnly the words were pronounced, 'Although I am in heaven, I am everywhere; for everywhere is heaven if I am there. I cannot suffer as I once suffered; but whenever my children are cold or hungry, or persecuted or neglected, I suffer with them; and whenever they are warm and fed, and sheltered and loved, I rejoice with them; so that Jesus is often cold, and Jesus is often warm.'"

There is need ofttimes for money, and those who have it must use it to relieve the needs of their suffering neighbors. Yet it should be remembered that the help which human lives need, in nine cases out of ten, is not money-help. "Silver and gold have I none," said Peter to the lame man at the Beautiful Gate, "but such as I have give I thee." And what he gave was infinitely better than gold or silver would have been. He said to him, "In the name of Jesus Christ of Nazareth, rise up and walk." Then, taking the lame man by the hand, he lifted him up; and at once his weak limbs became strong, so that he could walk alone, needing no longer to sit by the temple entrance, and ask for alms. Better help had been given him than any alms the poor man ever received.

This story is a parable as well as a fact. Its lesson is, that there are better things to give than gold and silver. If we can put new life and hope into the heart of a discouraged man, so that he rises out of his weak despair, and takes his place again in the ranks of active life, we have done a far better thing for him than if we had put our hands into our pockets, and given him money to help him nurse a little longer his miserable and unmanly despair. The truest sympathy is not that weak emotion which only sits down and weeps with a sufferer, imparting no courage or hope, but that wiser love, which, while it is touched by his pain and grief, and feels tenderly toward him, seeks to put new strength into his heart, to enable him to endure his suffering in a victorious way.

What most people really need in their troubles, is not to have the burden lifted off, or even lightened, but to have their own hearts strengthened with fresh cheer and hope, so that they shall not fail in their duty, and that they may overcome in their struggles. Not assistance in carrying the load, but a new inspiration of courage and energy, that they may carry it themselves, is for most men the wisest help. The true problem of living is not to get along easily, with the least exertion and the fewest crosses, but to grow by every experience into stronger men : hence we show real unkindness to those who are enduring hardship, when we seek merely to make life easier for them, regardless of their own highest good. Usually it is a great deal better for people to fight their own battles through, and carry their own burdens, and bear unlightened the crosses God gives them to carry. He knows better than we do what they need, and is ever watching, that the trial may not become more than they shall be able to bear. He will have relief ready when it is wisest that there should be relief. We may interfere with God's discipline when we come running up with our help at every moment of stress. By encouragement and cheer and inspiration, we may put new hope and energy into hearts that are fainting; but usually that is the only aid we should give. It is always vastly better to give a man something to do, by which he can earn his own bread, than to put the bread into his hand, and leave him idle. In the former case, we encourage him to be brave and manly: in the latter, we make it easy for him to be weak and despairing, and rob him of a lesson which God had set for him to learn. It is the poorest kindness to work out a child's school-examples for him, and to tell him the answers to the questions assigned to him. In doing so, we make the lessons of little or no use to him. The mere having of correct answers is a matter of small importance to him in comparison with the mental discipline to be gotten from the personal and even painful search after the truth. We can show him no greater unkindness than to make his lessons easy for him by doing all the hard part for him. The truly kind thing is, to encourage him to solve the examples, and to search out the answers for himself. Each bit of knowledge which he gets for himself through persistent struggle, he will keep forever. It is then his own, by virtue of search and discovery, and he will never lose it: besides, the wrestling with the hard problem has added new power to his own mental faculties, and the victory over the difficulty has inspired him with fresh hope for new struggles. The same is true in all spheres of life. We may do others the greatest harm by unwisely helping them. If having an easy life were the highest aim, it would be better that we should lift off every burden under which others bow, and do every hard thing for them, and save them from every struggle and difficulty. But life is a school, and tasks and hardships and battles and toils and sufferings are lessons set for us, by which we are to be trained and disciplined into strength and nobleness : therefore, he who tries only to make easy paths for another robs him of that experience by which God designed to make a man of him.

Hence, they are the best comforters and helpers of their fellow-men who go about with large hopefulness and cheerfulness in their own hearts, trying to put a little more hope and cheer into the life of every one they meet. Gifts of money, ofttimes, while they relieve immediate distress, and make life for one hour easier, only help to encourage disheartenment, and to perpetuate nervelessness and indolence. It would be a great deal better, by a few brave words, to incite the person to rise up, and grasp life anew, and conquer for himself.

It is evident, from this view of what is best for men, that we can all do a great deal of good, and of the wisest, truest good, in this world, without having much money to bestow. If we have not gold and silver to give, we can take by the hand those who have fallen in the way, and help them to rise again; we can put fresh courage into the hearts of the faint, so that they can take up their burdens afresh, and start forward once more in the race; we can give cheer and comfort to those who are weary through toil or through sorrow; we can impart inspirations of joy, and kindle new hope in the bosoms of those who have begun to lag behind; we can make life a little easier for every one we meet, not by taking any thing from his burden, but by making him more able to bear it. And in the end, although we may never be able to give a dollar of money to relieve distress, it may be seen that the blessings we have scattered, or have gotten into people's very lives, are far more in number, and greater in value, than if, with lavish hand, we had been dispensing gold and silver all along our years.

There is never an end of opportunities for such personal helpfulness as this. There is a rich, possible wayside ministry, for instance, made up of countless small courtesies, gentle words, mere passing touches on the lives of those we casually meet; impulses given by putting a little more warmth into our ordinary salutations; influences flowing directly or indirectly from the things we do, and the words we speak. For example, we meet a friend on the street, whose heart is heavy: we stop a moment in passing, to speak a word of thoughtful cheer and hope; and it sings in his breast all day, like a note of angel song. We walk a little way with a young man who is in danger of turning out of the path of safety, and we let fall a sincere word of kindly interest in him, or of affectionate warning, which may help to save him. Amid the busiest scenes, when engaged in the most momentous labors, we may yet carry on a never-ceasing ministry of personal helpfulness, whose results shall spring up like flowers in the path behind us, or echo in the hearts of others like notes of holy song, or glow in other lives in touches of radiant beauty.

It is related of Leonardo da Vinci, that in his boyhood, when he saw caged birds exposed for sale on the streets of Florence, he would buy them, and set them free. It was a rare trait in a boy, and spoke of a noble heart full of genuine sympathy. As we go about the streets, we find many caged birds which we may set free, imprisoned joys that we may liberate, by the power that is in us of helping others. Naturalists say that the stork, having most tenderly fed its young, will sail under them when they first attempt to fly, and, if they begin to fall, will bear them up, and support them; and that, when one stork is wounded by the sportsman, the able ones gather about it, put their wings under it, and try to carry it away. These instincts in the bird teach us the lesson of helpfulness. We should come up close to those who are in any way overburdened or weak or faint, and, putting our own strength underneath them, help them along; and when another fellow-being is wounded or crushed, whether by sorrow or by sin, it is our duty to gather about him, and try to lift him up, and save him. There is scarcely a limit to our possibilities of helpfulness in these ways.

"Poor indeed thou must be, if around thee
    Thou no ray of light and joy canst throw;
If no silken cord of love hath bound thee
    To some little world, through weal or woe;
If no dear eyes thy tender love can brighten,
    No fond voices answer to thine own;
If no brother's sorrow thou canst lighten
    By daily sympathy and gentle tone.
Daily struggling, though enclosed and lonely,
    Every day a rich reward will give:
Thou wilt find by hearty striving only,
    And truly loving, thou canst truly live!"

"There is a man," said his neighbor, speaking of the village carpenter, "who has done more good, I really believe, in this community than any other person who ever lived in it. He cannot talk very well in a prayer-meeting, and he doesn't often try. He isn't worth two thousand dollars, and it's very little he can put down on subscription-papers for any object. But a new family never moves into the village that he does not find them out, to give them a neighborly welcome, and to offer any little service he can render. He is always on the look-out to give strangers a seat in his pew at church. He is always ready to watch with a sick neighbor, and look after his affairs for him. I have sometimes thought, that he and his wife keep house-plants in winter just to be able to send flowers to invalids. He finds time for a pleasant word for every child he meets; and you'll see the children climbing into his own one-horse wagon, when he has no other load. He really seems to have a genius for helping folks in all sorts of common ways, and it does me good every day just to meet him on the street." This picture, though in homely setting, it may do some one good to look at; so it is framed here, and left on this page.

Thus, without money, we can make our lives abundantly useful in this world of need. Sympathy is better than money: so is courage, so is cheer, so is hope. It is better always to give ourselves than to give our money: certainly we should give ourselves with whatever else we may give. "The gift without the giver is bare." Christ himself gave no money; but every life that came near to him in faith, went away enriched and helped. He gave love, and love is the brightest and richest coin minted in this world. And all of us can give love : none are too poor for that.

CHAPTER XVI.

TIMELINESS IN DUTY.

THE element of time is a vital matter in many duties. Done at the right moment, there is a blessing in them; delayed, they were as well not done at all. If we sleep through the hour for duty, we may as well sleep on after the hour. Waking then will not avail to accomplish that which we were set to do.

There are many applications of this principle. Whatever we do for our friends, we must do when they need our help. If one is sick, the time to show our affection and our sympathy is while the sickness continues, and not after the friend is well again. If we allow him to pass through his illness without showing him any attention, there is no use, when he is going about again, for us to wake up, and begin to lavish kindness upon him: he does not need it now, and it will do him no good.

If one of our friends is passing through some sore struggle with temptation, and is in danger of being overcome, then is the time to come up close alongside of him, and put the strength of our love under his weakness to support him. If we fail him then, we may almost as well let him go on alone altogether after that. Of what use is sympathy when the struggle is over? Of what use is help when the battle has been fought through, and won without us? Or, suppose the friend was not victorious; suppose he failed in the battle, — failed because no one came to him to help him, because *we* came not with the sustaining strength of our sympathy; suppose that, left to struggle unaided with enemies or difficulties or adversities, he was defeated, and sank down crushed and hopeless, — is there any use in our hurrying up to him now to proffer our assistance? Is not the time past when help could avail him? Can our sympathy now enable him to retrieve what he has lost? Can our faithfulness to-day atone for our unfaithfulness yesterday?

Most of us are in some way the guardians of

other souls. The time to fulfil our duty of guardianship is when the dangers are imminent. There is no use for the look-out on the ship to become vigilant only after the vessel is among the rocks. There is no use for the sentinel, in the time of war, to arouse and begin to watch when the enemy has stolen in and captured the field.

Are you your brother's keeper? Are you set to watch against danger to his soul? Are you a parent, whose duty it is to guard your own children against the perils of sin that lurk in ambush all about them? Are you a teacher, with a class of young people intrusted to your care, to shield and train and keep? Are you a sister, with brothers dear to you, whom you are to protect from temptation? Are you a brother, and have you sisters tender and exposed to danger, whose defender you should be? Are you a friend, and is there one beset by perils, over whom God has set you as guide or protector? Are you watching, or are you sleeping? Remember that the time to watch is before the danger has done its deadly work.

When, through your negligence, it has come, and has destroyed the precious life, you may almost as well sleep on. Watching then ever so faithfully will not undo the evil which is done.

In the preparation for duty or for struggle in our personal life, the same principle applies. There is a time for this preparation, when it can be made; and if it is not made then, it cannot be made at all. It is a rule of providential leading, that opportunity is always given to every one to prepare for whatever part he is to take in life, and for whatever experience he is ordained to meet. The days come to us linked one to another, so that simple faithfulness to-day always prepares us for the duty of to-morrow. Or the days are like steps on a stairway, each one meant to lift our feet, and make us ready for the next. If one only embraces and uses his opportunities as they come to him, one by one, he will never be surprised by any sudden emergency in life, whether of duty or of trial, for which he will not be ready. For example, before life's stern, fierce conflicts, which put manhood's strongest fibre to the test, we have childhood and youth as seasons for calm preparation. He that rightly improves these seasons is fully ready for whatever life may bring.

It is just because these opportunities for preparation come to us so quietly, and without announcement, not recognized by us at the time as important, or as carrying in them any elements of destiny for us, that so many fail to improve them. The school-boy does not see what good it will do him to know the simple things that are set as his daily tasks, and neglects to learn them. Twenty, forty years afterward, he fails in the position to which he is called, because he slurred his boyhood lessons in the quiet school-days long ago. The young apprentice takes no pains to perfect himself in the trade he has chosen, and consequently is only a third or fourth class workman all his life, while diligence in youth would have prepared him for highest excellence. The young professional man dislikes the dry drudgery that the early years bring to him, and neglects it, waiting until some great opportunity comes to lift him into prominence. The opportunity comes at length, but he fails in it, because he has not improved the long series of preparatory steps that came before.

On the other hand, a school-boy does every task faithfully. He never slights a lesson; he goes thoroughly over every day's studies; he does not see, any more than the other, of what particular use these things will be to him when he is a man, in active life, nor does he ask: his only care is to be faithful now in every duty. Years later he rises to high places which he never could have filled had he slurred his boyhood's tasks. A physician is suddenly called to take charge of a critical case, requiring the best skill in the world. He is successful, and wins fame for himself, because in the long, quiet years of obscure practice he has been diligent. If he had not been faithful in those years of routine work, he must have failed when the great opportunity came. He could not have made the necessary preparation at the moment when suddenly called to act. The case could only be met by the instant use of knowledge and skill already acquired and available.

It is a secret worth knowing and remembering, that the truest, and indeed the only possible, preparation for life's duties or trials, is made by simple fidelity in whatever each day brings. A day squandered anywhere may prove the dropped stitch from which the whole web will begin to ravel. One lesson neglected may prove to have contained the very knowledge for the want of which, far along in the course, the student may fail. One opportunity let slip may be the first step in a ladder leading to eminence or power, but no higher rounds of which can be gained, because the first was not taken. We never know what is important, or when we are standing at the open doors of great opportunities, in life. The most insignificant duty that offers may be the first lesson in preparation for a noble mission : if we despise or neglect it, we miss the grand destiny, the gate to which was open just for that one moment. Indeed, every hour of life holds the keys of the next, and possibly of many hours more: to fail of our duty in any one of them, may be to lose the most splendid opportunity through all life to the end.

So the times of preparation come silently and unawares; and many neglect them, not knowing what depends upon them: but neglected, and allowed to slip away, they can never be regained. The man who finds himself in the presence of a great duty or opportunity which he cannot take up or accept, because he is not prepared for it, cannot then go back to make the needful preparation. The soldier cannot learn the art of war in the face of the battle. The Christian cannot, in an unexpected emergency of temptation, gather in a moment all needed spiritual power. Not to be ready in advance for great duties or great needs, is to fail.

The lesson is important, and has infinite applications. You cannot go back to-day to do the work you neglected to do yesterday. You cannot make preparation for life when the burden of life is on you. Opportunities never return. They must be taken on the wing, or they cannot be taken at all. There is a time for every duty; done then, its issues and results may be infinite and eternal: deferred or neglected, it may never be worth while to take it up again.

> "Muffled and dumb, the hypocritic days,
> And marching single in an endless file,
> Bring diadems or fagots in their hands.
> To each they offer gifts after his will, —
> Bread, kingdoms, stars, and heaven that holds them all.
> I, in my pleachèd garden, watched the pomp,
> Forgot my morning wishes, hastily
> Took a few herbs and apples, and the day
> Turned and departed silent: I, too late,
> Under her solemn fillet saw the scorn."

Many of us in our later years have in our hands only the poorest things of life, — withered leaves, faded flowers, straws, and bits of worthless tinsel, while we can see afar in their bright glory the kingdoms, diadems, and crowns which we have missed, which might have been ours had we but taken them when they were offered to us. Let the young learn the lesson, and miss no chance that life brings, and refuse no blessing which the commonest day presents, in whatever plainness of form. It may be only a dull, dry little seed which is held out to you, but in it is infolded a rare, sweet flower, which some day will fill your room with fragrance, if you accept it: you cannot have the flower then unless you take the seed to-day.

CHAPTER XVII.

THE OFFICE OF CONSOLER.

"For she is kinder than all others are,
   And weak things, sad things, gather where she dwells,
  To reach and taste her strength, and drink of her,
   As thirsty creatures of clear water-wells."

THERE are some people who seem to be specially anointed to the office of comforter and consoler. The sorrowing and troubled are attracted to them as steel filings to a magnet, or as thirsty ones to a spring of water. The paths to their doors are worn by the passing feet of many weary ones. No office among men is more sacred, or fuller of blessing; for in no other field can wider opportunity be found for rendering helpful service to humanity. It was to this service, in an eminent degree, that Christ was set apart. He said of himself, that the Spirit had sent him "to heal the broken-hearted." His whole ministry was one of consolation to the sorrowing. The weary and the heartsore came to him with their burdens; the penitent crept to his feet with their confessions; mourners sought his sympathy: and, wherever he went, he carried cheer, light, and inspiration. No one who came to him with a trouble went away uncomforted. His deep and ready sympathy and his gentle, uplifting help made him pre-eminently a consoler.

Those who would follow in Christ's footsteps, and repeat in their human measure his ministry of love and beneficence in this world, must strive to be sons of consolation. There is always need for this sacred ministry. Wherever one may live, there is no other human experience that one is so sure of meeting as sorrow. In other respects men differ, — in race, in color, in worldly condition, in culture, in degrees of refinement, in customs and modes of life, — but in one respect all are alike: all have sorrow. There are many languages spoken on the earth, and the traveller ofttimes finds himself unable to understand the word that falls upon his ear; but there is one language that he finds the same in all zones, in all conditions, — the language of grief. Everywhere there are tears telling of sadness. There is no circle in which there is not some heavy heart. We pass no day in which we do not meet with those who are oppressed with some open or secret grief. An old clergyman once said to a company of students he was addressing, that they ought never to conduct a religious service without some word of comfort for the troubled, for they would always have some troubled ones in their audience. Wherever we go, we come upon those who long for sympathy, and whose hearts are crying out for comfort.

Therefore, those who have learned to comfort others have found a ministry of great usefulness. It was the early prayer of Mrs. Prentiss, who has helped so many weary pilgrims heavenward, —

"Oh that this heart, with grief so well acquainted,
  Might be a fountain, rich and sweet and full,
For all the weary that have fallen and fainted
  In life's parched desert, — thirsty, sorrowful.

> Thou Man of sorrows, teach my lips, that often
>   Have told the sacred story of my woe,
> To speak of thee till stony griefs I soften, —
>   Till those that know thee not, learn thee to know."

Her prayer was answered; for of this gifted woman, after her death, it was said with great truthfulness, "Hers was in an eminent degree the blessing of them that were ready to perish. Weary, overtaxed mothers, misunderstood and unappreciated wives, servants, pale seamstresses, delicate women forced to live in an atmosphere of drunkenness and coarse brutality, widows and orphans in the bitterness of their bereavement, mothers with their tears dropping over empty cradles, — to thousands of such she was a messenger from heaven." To receive such eulogium when one's work is finished, is better than to have died amid the richest splendors of wealth, or to have had the pæans of fame sung over one's grave.

The anointing to the office of consoler is usually an anointing of tears. Only those who have learned in God's school of experience can be the best comforters of others. It was thus that Christ himself was prepared to be the great Comforter. It is because on earth he was tried in all points as we are, that now in heaven he is touched with the feeling of our infirmities. Even his divinity did not qualify him for sympathy: he must learn by actual human experience what sorrow is, that he might be the comforter of sorrow. It is in the same school that God ordinarily trains his children for this sacred office. He may not take them through bereavements (Christ did not suffer bereavements), but there are many other kinds of suffering in which hearts may be schooled. Some learn their lessons in early struggles with adversity, or with temptation, or with the weakness and sin of their own natures, or in disappointments, self-denials, and trials. Many who seem to common eyes to have escaped the sorrows of life, have yet in many ways been trained and disciplined, and their hearts chastened and softened, and cleansed of the hardness and selfishness of nature; so that they are well prepared to understand the experiences of others in struggle and sorrow, and give true and wise consolation. This is one of the rich compensations of trial: we get out of it, if we endure it Christianly, preparation for one of life's most sacred ministries.

As to the manner in which this ministry of consolation may be performed, but few suggestions can be made. If the heart is ready for it, no rules will be needed. Genuine sympathy is the basis of all true and wise comfort. We must enter into the experiences of those to whom we would minister comfort; we must understand their grief: this will make us reverent in the presence of their trouble. If we could read the secret history of those about us, who now ofttimes try our patience by their infelicities of temper and disposition, we should probably find in their lives sorrow and suffering enough to explain to us the infirmities which so mar their character. True sympathy draws us very close to the sufferer. It also gives us that thoughtfulness, and that delicacy of feeling and touch, which make us gentle in all our treatment of grief; for no other ministry is refinement of spirit so essential as for that of dealing

THE OFFICE OF CONSOLER. 187

with pained or wounded hearts. A wrong touch, or a harsh word, or the quick flash of an eye, may do irreparable harm, only opening afresh, with new pain and torture, the wound it was meant to heal. Hence, there is deep significance in the prophet's portraiture of Christ's gentleness in dealing with crushed spirits: "A bruised reed shall he not break." He never caused needless pain to the bruised heart he meant to soothe. No touch of his was ever rude: no word of his was ever harsh. We need, in like manner, the most delicate gentleness for the offices of comfort.

We need also victorious faith, as well as gentleness, to fit us for the ministry of consolation. We cannot give what we have not ourselves to give. How can we communicate strong faith in God and in his Word, if our own hearts are full of doubts and misgivings? How can we kindle the lamps of hope and courage and joy in the heart where all is dark, if there be no lamps shining in our own breast? A true comforter must know deep Christian joy, — the joy that springs up amid sorrows, like a sweet, fresh spring under the tides of the brackish sea. One woman wrote to another in deep grief, "The shadow of death will not always rest on your home : you will emerge from its obscurity into such a light as they who have never sorrowed cannot know. We never know, or begin to know, the great Heart that loves us best, till we throw ourselves upon it in the hour of our despair." This writer herself knew the joy which she foretold to her sister, now walking in the deep shadow. One who had had sorrow, but had never gotten out into the sunshine, could not have given such comfort. Bright, radiant, victorious faith is essential in one who would give real consolation. One who has not come as a conqueror through Christ out of affliction, but has been crushed, and still lies in the dust of defeat, cannot minister comfort to others. A vanquished soldier cannot inspire courage and hope in another who is going out to battle. We must be overcomers ourselves, if we would help others to overcome. We must be truly comforted of God, if we would comfort others.

THE OFFICE OF CONSOLER. 189

As to the quality of the comfort itself that is ministered, it should be more than pity. Mere pity alone leaves the heart weaker than before. Wise and true comfort must give something that shall prove strength and inspiration to the fainting spirit, and help it to rise again. It should be like the wine which angels of mercy pour into the lips of the wounded on the fields of battle to revive them. The design of comfort is not merely to help the sorrowing through their sorrow, but to help them to get from their sorrow the blessing it has for them, to take from God the message of love which the sorrow bears, and to come from the experience stronger, purer, more radiant, with more of Christ's image glowing in their face.

Wise and really helpful comfort, while it is touched by the friend's sorrow, and shares the pain, yet strives to put hope and strength into the sad heart, that recognizing God's hand, and submitting to it, it may yet take the benediction which the dark-robed messenger brings. In no experience of life do most persons need wise friendship and firm guidance more than in their times of trouble. There are dangerous shoals skirting all the deeps of affliction, and many frail barks are wrecked in the darkness. It is the office of the one who would give good comfort, to pilot the sorrowing past the shoals to the safe and radiant shore. For this, a firm hand is needed as well as a tender heart.

CHAPTER XVIII.

LIVING BY THE DAY.

> "Time *was*, is past: thou canst not it recall.
> Time *is*, thou hast: employ the portion small.
> Time *future*, is not, and may never be.
> Time present is the only time for thee."

IT is life's largeness that most discourages earnest and conscientious souls. As men think deeply of its meaning and responsibility, they are apt to be overwhelmed by the thought of its vastness. It has manifold, almost infinite, relations toward God and toward man. Each of these relations has its binding duties. Every individual life must be lived amid countless antagonisms, and in the face of countless perils. Battles must be fought, trials encountered, and sorrows endured. Every life has a divine mission to fulfil, a plan of God to work out. Then the brief earthly course is but the beginning of an endless existence, whose immortal destinies hinge upon fidelity in the present life. Looked at in this way, as a whole, there is something almost appalling in the thought of our responsibility in living.

Many a person who thinks of life in this aspect, and sees it in its wholeness, has not the courage to hope for success and victory, but stands staggered, well-nigh paralyzed, on the threshold. "I cannot possibly meet all these responsibilities, and perform all these duties. I can but fail in the end if I try: why should I try at all, only to suffer the shame and pain of defeat?" Despair comes to many a heart when either duty or sorrow or danger is looked at in the aggregate.

But this is not the way we should view life. It does not come to us all in one piece. We do not get it even in years, but only in days,— day by day. We look on before us, and as we count up the long years with their duties, struggles, and trials, the bulk is like a mountain which no mortal can carry; but we really never have more than one day's battles to fight, or one day's work to do, or one day's burdens to bear, or one day's sorrow to endure, in any one day.

> " I think not of to-morrow,
> Its trial or its task,
> But still with childlike spirit
> For present mercies ask.
> With each returning morning
> I cast old things away.
> Life's journey lies before me:
> My prayer is for to-day."

It is wonderful how the Bible gives emphasis to this way of viewing life. When for forty years God fed his chosen people with bread from heaven, he never gave them, except on the morning before the sabbath, more than one day's portion at a time. He positively forbade them gathering more than would suffice for the day, and if they should violate his command, what they gathered over the daily portion would become corrupt. Thus early God began to teach his people to live only by the day, and trust him for to-morrow. At the close of the forty years, the promise given to one of the tribes was, "As thy days, so shall thy strength be." Strength was not promised in advance, — enough for all life, or even for a year, or for a month, — but the promise was, that for each day, when it came with its own needs, duties, battles, and griefs, enough strength would be given. As the burden increased, more strength would be imparted. As the night grew darker, the lamps would shine out more brightly. The important thought here is, that strength is not emptied into our hearts in bulk, — a supply for years to come, — but is kept in reserve, and given day by day, just as the day's needs require.

> "Oh! ask not thou, How shall I bear
> The burden of to-morrow?
> Sufficient for to-day, its care,
> Its evil, and its sorrow;
> God imparteth *by the way*
> Strength sufficient for the day."

When Christ came, he gave still further emphasis to the same method of living. He said, "Be not anxious for the morrow; for the morrow will be anxious for itself. Sufficient unto the day is the evil thereof." He would have us fence off the days by themselves, and never look over the fence to think about to-morrow's cares. The thought is, that each day is, in a certain sense, a complete life by itself. It has its own duties, its own trials, its own burdens, and its own needs. It has enough to fill heart and hands for the one full day. We cannot live its life well, and use any of its strength outside of itself. The very best we can do for any day, for the perfecting of our life as a whole, is to live the one day well. We should put all our thought and energy and skill into the duty of each day, wasting no strength, either in grieving over yesterday's failures, or in anxiety about to-morrow's responsibilities.

> "Bear the burden of the present,
>   Let the morrow bear its own:
> If the morning sky be pleasant,
>   Why the coming night bemoan?
>
> Grief, nor pain, nor any sorrow,
>   Rends thy heart to Him unknown:
> He to-day and He to-morrow
>   Grace sufficient gives His own."

Charles Kingsley says, "Do to-day's duty, fight to-day's temptation, and do not weaken and distract yourself by looking forward to things which you cannot see, and could not understand if you saw them."

Our Lord, also, in the form of prayer which he gave his disciples, taught this lesson of living by the day. There he has told us to ask for bread for one day only. "Give us this day our daily bread." Here, again, he teaches us that we have to do only with the present day. We do not need to-morrow's bread now: when we need it, it will be soon enough to ask God for it, and get it. It is the manna lesson over again. God is caring for us, and we are to trust him for the supply of all our wants as they press upon us: we are to trust him, content to have only enough in hand for the day.

> "Why should'st thou fill to-day with sorrow
>   About to-morrow,
>   My heart?
>   One watches all with care most true:
>   Doubt not that He will give thee, too,
>   Thy part"

If we can but learn to live thus by the day, without anxiety about the future, the burden will not be so crushing. We have nothing to do with life in the aggregate, — that great bulk of duties, responsibilities, struggles, and trials that belong to a course of years. We really have nothing to do even with the nearest of the days before us, — to-morrow. Our sole business is with the one little day now passing. And *its* burdens will not crush us: we can easily carry them till the sun goes down. We can get along for one short day : it is the projection of life into the long future that dismays and appals us. So the lesson makes life easy and simple.

> "One day at a time. Every heart that aches
>   Knows only too well how long that can seem ;
> But it's never to-day which the spirit breaks, —
>   It's the darkened future, without a gleam.
>
> One day at a time. A burden too great
>   To be borne for two can be borne for one :
> Who knows what will enter to-morrow's gate ?
>   While yet we are speaking, all may be done.

> One day at a time. But a single day,
>   Whatever its load, whatever its length ;
> And there's a bit of precious Scripture to say,
>   That according to each shall be our strength."

But is there to be no forethought? The best forethought for to-morrow is to-day's duty well done. It is so in school: one lesson well learned leads up to the next, and makes it easy; and each day's lessons mastered through the years, give scholarship in the end. It is so in all life: if to-day is well lived, if all its responsibilities are promptly and wisely met, to-morrow will come bright with new hopes. God gives guidance, also, by the day. One who carries a lantern at night does not see the whole path home; the lantern lights only a single step in advance; but, when that step is taken, another is thereby lighted, and so on until the end of the journey is reached. It is thus that God lights our way. He does not show us the whole of it when we set out: he makes one step plain, and then, when we take that, another and then another.

"If thou hast yesterday thy duty done,
　　And thereby cleared firm footing for to-day,
　Whatever clouds may dark to-morrow's sun,
　　Thou shalt not miss thy solitary way."

CHAPTER XIX.

HABITS IN RELIGIOUS LIFE.

> " Forenoon and afternoon and night; — forenoon
> And afternoon and night; — forenoon and — what!
> The empty song repeats itself. No more?
> Yea, that is life: make this forenoon sublime,
> This afternoon a psalm, this night a prayer,
> And time is conquered, and thy crown is won."
> E. R. Sill.

SOME conscientious people are anxious because their religious life has become such a matter of habit, that they are not conscious of any voluntary efforts to live right. They feel that their acts and services cannot be pleasing to God when rendered without any conscious desire to honor him. They are oppressed with the fear that their comfortable religion is really only formality. They pray at certain hours, and go to church at certain times, and they go through regular routines of duties, and they seem to be good and to do good by routine rather than from the heart. The methodicalness of their piety frightens them when they think seriously about it: it seems to them, that, in all their acts of devotion and service, there should be a spontaneous feeling, ever fresh and sweet.

A little reflection will show us that such anxiety is groundless. All true greatness is unconscious of itself. It is so of beauty. The sweetest feature in childhood is its unconsciousness. Whenever the little girl begins to be conscious that she is pretty, her beauty is greatly marred. The highest skill in any art is that which is not conscious of skill. Poets do their best work when they are conscious of no effort. They write, as it were, by natural inspiration, just as a bird sings. Artists reach their highest achievements when they are conscious of making no great exertion. A musician brings the sweetest strains from his instrument when he is not conscious of trying to do any thing great. The highest attainment in any art is that in which the art is forgotten. The appearance of effort mars any performance.

All truly great things are done easily and unconsciously.

The principle is just as true in its application to Christian life. When one is conscious of his spiritual graces, the beauty of these graces is marred. When a man knows that he is humble, his humility vanishes. When one has to make efforts to be generous, patient, or unselfish, he has yet much to learn about these elements. The highest reach in Christian character brings the disciple back to the simplicity of a little child, when he is utterly unconscious of the splendor of his character in Heaven's sight.

This is the culmination, but it takes many years ofttimes to attain to such completeness. Take piano-playing. You listen entranced to the skilful performer. His fingers fly over the keys, and wander over the chords, up and down the octaves, and the music thrills you. You are utterly amazed at the skill he exhibits: yet it seems no effort to him; he does it all as easily as the bird sings its morning song in the grove. This is the ultimate of his art; but it was not always so. Back of what you now see and hear, lie long, patient years of weary, toilsome learning, and tedious, exhausting practice, when he had to pick out each separate note on the key-board, then pass to the next, and search for that.

So you see a Christian who is very patient, or has great meekness. He is not easily provoked. When he is insulted, his face grows a little pale, but there is no outburst; no anger clouds his brow; no passionate word escapes his lips; he rules his own spirit; he speaks the soft answer, or is silent; or, he has wondrous Christian joy. He has sorrows, but amid them all his heart rejoices. His life is a "song in the night," or he has attained rare, almost unearthly, spirituality. He seems to have actual converse with heaven. A celestial brightness clings to him. He walks the earth as if he were a visitant from another world; his daily life is a prayer, breathing out a silent, unconscious influence of heavenliness, as a sweet flower pours out fragrance on the common air; or he lives a Christian life of superior nobleness. He displays the graces of the spirit in unusual measure. He manifests Christ's hidden life wherever he goes. His life is one of great usefulness, as, with beautiful unselfishness, he ministers to the good of others. His heart is touched by every cry of distress, and his hand goes out to give relief to all suffering and need; and all this costs no effort. It appears easy and natural for him to be just such a Christian, and he seems unconscious of any pre-eminent attainments.

Looking at such characters and lives, many feel discouraged. They say, "I can never be such a Christian;" or perhaps they take another view of it, and say, "It costs these men or women nothing to be good Christians: it is easy and natural to them. They have to make no effort to be true, meek, gentle, unselfish, or good-tempered and sweet-spirited. If they had my quick, fiery nature, they could not be so; if they were made of tinder, as I am, they would not be able so to rule their spirits under keen provocation; if they had my strong feelings, they could not be joyful when sorrow sweeps over them; if they had all my peculiarities of constitution, circumstance, and environment, all my trials and difficulties, they could not be such lovely, full-rounded Christians."

No doubt, there is something in temperament and constitution, but there is far less than many of us claim. It is very convenient to have such a scapegoat on which to pile the responsibility for bad temper and execrable living, but the difference usually is in the culture of the life. It is just as in the case of the pianist. You see the matured character, the disciplined spirit, the trained life; and you marvel at the ease, the perfectness, the unconsciousness, with which these beautiful things are done; but you know nothing of the years that lie back of these results, in which there were exertions, efforts, struggles, and failures, amid which, a thousand times, hearts grew faint, and spirits sank almost in despair. What we admire and envy in the finely cultured character, is not the spontaneity of unschooled nature, but the result of years and years of patient and painful discipline, by which a disposition, perhaps coarse and rude and impetuous, has been trained into refinement, gentleness, and calm peace.

The tendency of all faithful and true living is toward the confirmation and solidifying of character. We grow always in the direction of our habits and efforts. He that continually struggles to be unselfish, will have many a conflict and many a defeat; but at length he will learn to exercise an unselfish spirit without any exertion. The wheels have run so long and so often in one track, that they have cut deep grooves for themselves, into which they fall as if by nature. Yet this does not take away from the moral character of the acts themselves. Indeed, it shows, that, instead of doing certain specific things in detail to please God, the whole life has become bent, trained, and solidified into conformity with right. It shows, that, instead of piecemeal obedience, holy principles have become wrought into the very fibre and quality of the soul. There may be less feeling, less emotion, less consciousness of trying to please God in the minute acts of life; but the character itself has taken on the stamp of holiness, and the natural motions of the soul have been trained into the grooves of righteousness. Yielding habitually to the monitions of the Spirit, the life has been transformed more and more into the image of Christ, until unconsciously, and without effort, the Christian does the things that please God.

This is the ultimate of Christian culture. It has in the highest and truest sense become "second nature" to do right and beautiful things, and not even to stop to think of them as right and beautiful, or to weigh their moral character. Who does not know some quiet Christian life that makes no pretension to greatness, that is simple, humble, modest, retiring, and yet performs a blessed ministry, breathing fragrance and joy all about itself? The more we watch the seeds which grow and bring forth fruit in this world, the more shall we learn that they are oftenest those that are unconsciously dropped, when the sower knows not that his hand is scattering golden grains of life. When we try to do something great or fine, nothing comes of it. God seems to blight the things we do with large intent: then, when we do some simple thing, without pretentious purpose, or any thought of excellence or fame, he makes the results immortal. Surely no one will say that these beautiful things possess no moral quality, because they are wrought unconsciously, or through force of long habit.

A ripe Christian character is simply a life in which all Christian virtues and graces have become fixed and solidified into permanence as established habits. It costs no struggle to do right, because what has been done so long, under the influence of grace in the heart, has become part of the regenerated nature. The bird sings not to be heard, but because the song is in its heart, and must be expressed. It sings just as sweetly in the depths of the wood, with no ear to listen, as by the crowded thoroughfare. Beethoven did not sing for fame, but to give utterance to the glorious music that filled his soul. The face of Moses did not shine to convince the people of his holiness, but because he had dwelt so long in the presence of God that it could not but shine. Truest, ripest Christian life flows out of a full heart, — a heart so filled with Christ that it requires no effort to live well, and to scatter the sweetness of grace and love.

It must be remembered, however, that all goodness in living begins first in obeying rules, in keeping commandments. Mozart and Mendelssohn began with running scales and striking chords, and with painful finger-exercises. The noblest Christian began with the simplest obediences. The way to become skilful is to do things over and over, until we can do them perfectly, and without thought or effort. The way to become able to do great things, is to do our little things with endless repetition, and with increasing dexterity and carefulness. The way to grow into Christlikeness of character, is to watch ourselves in the minutest things of thought and word and act, until our powers are trained to go almost without watching in the lines of moral right and holy beauty. To become prayerful, we must learn to pray by the clock, at fixed times. It is fine ideal talk to say that our devotions should be like the bird's songs, warbling out anywhere, and at any time, with sweet unrestraint; but in plain truth, to depend upon such impulses as guides to praying, would soon lead to no praying at all. This may do for our heavenly life; but we have not gotten into heaven yet, and until we do, we need to pray by habit. So of all religious life. We can only grow into patience by being as patient as we can, daily and hourly, and in smallest matters, ever learning to be more and more patient until we reach the highest possible culture in that line. We can only become unselfish by practising unselfishness wherever we have an opportunity, until our life grows into the permanent beauty of unselfishness. We can only grow better by striving ever to be better than we already are, and by climbing step by step toward the radiant heights of excellence. "We become better than we are by doing better than it is in our heart to do, better than it is yet our new nature to do. . . . The quickest way to outgrow rule, is to make faithful use of rule. The melted iron can dispense with the mould by having been run in the mould. . The more pains we take to make the letters in our copy-book like those at the top of the page, the sooner we can get along without any copy-book. The element of the formal and the mechanical is the threshold over which we step forward to any new acquisition."

> "Slowly fashioned, link by link,
>   Slowly waxing strong,
> 'Till the spirit never shrink,
>   Save from touch of wrong.
>
> Holy habits are thy wealth,
>   Golden, pleasant chains, —
> Passing earth's prime blessing, health, —
>   Endless, priceless gains.
>
> Holy habits are thy joy,
>   Wisdom's pleasant ways,
> Yielding good without alloy,
>   Lengthening, too, thy days."

Thus our daily habits carry in them the buds and prophecies of our future character. The test of all moral life is in its *tendencies*. The question is not, What point have you attained? but, Which way are you tending? In what direction is your growth? Is your character compacting toward patience, gentleness, truth, love? or toward impatience, hardness, falsehood, and selfishness? What is the trend of your spiritual habits? We grow always in the direction of our daily living. The powers we use develop continually into greater strength. The graces we cultivate come out more and more clearly in our character. A bird that would not use its wings would soon have no wings that it could use. Made to soar above the earth as our souls are, to fly toward God and heaven, if we only grovel in the dust, and do not use our wings, we lose power to soar, and our whole life grows toward earthliness. But if we train ourselves to look upward, to walk erect, to gather our soul's food from the branches of the tree of life, our whole being will grow toward spirituality and heavenliness.

CHAPTER XX.

THE POWER OF THE TONGUE.

> "Words are mighty, words are living
> Serpents with their venomed stings,
> Or bright angels crowding round us,
> With heaven's light upon their wings;
> Every word has its own spirit,
> True or false, that never dies;
> Every word man's lips have uttered,
> Lives on record in the skies."

"DEATH and life," says the wise man's proverb, "are in the power of the tongue." Words seem little things, so fleeting and evanescent, that apparently it cannot matter much of what sort they are. They are so easily spoken, that we forget what power they have to give pleasure or pain. They seem so swiftly gone after they have passed the door of our lips, and to have vanished so utterly, that we forget they do not really go away at all, but linger, either like barbed arrows in the heart where they struck, or, like fragrant flowers, distilling perfume. They seem to us, as we carelessly speak them, to be insignificant, and powerless for good or ill; and we do not stop to think, that, as they fly, they either tear down or build up fair fabrics of joy and peace in the souls of those to whom we speak. There have been words quietly spoken, which have broken like the lightning-flash, bearing sad desolation on their blighting wings, which years could not repair. On the other hand, there have been simple words which, treasured in memory, have hung like bright stars of joy and cheer in long, dark nights of sorrow and trial.

The tongue's power to do good is simply incalculable. It can impart valuable knowledge; it can speak words that will shine like lamps in darkened hearts; it can pronounce kindly sentences that will comfort sorrow, or cheer despondency; it can breathe thoughts that will arouse, inspire, and quicken heedless souls, and even whisper the divine secret of life-giving energy to spirits that are dead. What good we could do with our tongues, if we would use them to the full limit of their power for good, no one can compute. And these opportunities do not lie alone in formal speech, as in the sermon or the lesson, or in the occasional serious talk, but they come in all conversation, even in the most casual greeting on the street.

> "A kindly word and a tender tone, —
> To only God is their virtue known;
> They can lift from the dust the abject head,
> They can turn a foe to a friend instead;
> The heart close-barred with passion and pride
> Will fling at their knock its portal wide;
> And the hate that blights, and the scorn that sears,
> Will melt in the fountain of childlike tears.
>   What ice-bound barriers have been broken,
>   What rivers of love been stirred,
>   By a word in kindness spoken,
>   By only a gentle word."

But are these fine possibilities of speech realized by most people? Is the daily talk, even of fairly good men and women, a ministry of blessing and good to those on whose ears it falls? What is the staple of conversation among average Christians? Let us listen for a day, and make careful note of all we hear. How much of it is worth recording? How many sentences are spiritually helpful, calculated to kindle higher aspirations, or start upward impulses? How much of it is utterly empty, mere chaff, that feeds no heart-hunger, kindles no joy, helps no one to live better? How much is careless scandal, unjust and injurious criticism of the absent? How much is hypocritical and insincere?

It is startling to think what Christian conversation might be, of what it ought to be, and then of what it is. Why should such a power for good be wasted, or far worse than wasted? Why should our Christian development be retarded by the misuse of the marvellous gift of speech? It were far better that one were born dumb than that, having a tongue, one should use it to scatter evil and sorrow, or to sow the seeds of bitterness and pain. Our Lord said we must give account of every idle word; and, if for the idle words, how much more for the words that stain and injure, or fall as a destructive blight into other hearts and lives!

When we give ourselves to Christ, we ought to give him our tongues : when we are regenerated, our tongues ought to be regenerated. It was not without significance, that, when the Holy Ghost came down on the day of Pentecost, the manifestation was in "*tongues* like as of fire." One of the first results, too, of this heavenly baptism was that the disciples spoke with other tongues. It is not a mere fanciful interpretation that sees in all this an intimation that true conversation transforms the speech, and that a Christian should speak with a new Christian tongue.

There are many suggestions in the Scriptures as to the kind of words a Christian tongue should speak. For example: "Let no corrupt communication proceed out of your mouth, but that which is good to the use of edifying, that it may minister grace unto the hearers." Two essential features of Christian speech are here touched upon. One is purity: no corrupt word should ever fall from a consecrated tongue, yet there is much impurity in the speech of some professing Christians. Filthy stories are told, and there are vile allusions and innuendoes which stain the lips that utter them and the heart of him who hears. Christian conversation should be clean and white as snow. Nothing should be spoken in any company which could not be spoken in the presence of the most refined ladies. Will our every-day speech stand this test? The other quality indicated in this quotation is edification and the imparting of grace. Purity is only negative, that which does not stain and soil; but more is required. No sentence should be spoken which is not good for edifying, which does not minister grace. Every word should be fitted in some way to build up character, and add to its beauty. The geologist will take you to what was once the shore of an ancient sea, and show you the marks made by the patter of the raindrops on the soft sand, or the lines left by the wash of the waves. A leaf fluttered down from a tree, and fell there, imprinting its delicate figure. Ages have passed since that time, but every trace remains as perfect as when it was first made: the wash of the surf, the indentations made by the pattering raindrops, the minutest lines, the leaf's skeleton, — there they are, preserved through millenniums of years. So it is that words fall upon a human heart. Our gentle poet's thought is no idle fancy that the song he sings, he will find again long, long afterward, in the heart of his friend. Words uttered, fall and are forgotten as their echoes die away, but they leave their mark: they either beautify or mar; they either make the life brighter, or they sully it; they either build up, or they tear down what before was builded. A warm breath upon the mystic frost-work on the window-pane on a winter's morning causes all the splendor to vanish. So, before the breath of impure words, the soul's glory melts into ruin. The Christian's speech should always edify, and give grace; yet on how many lips, now garrulous with flippant words, would this test lay the finger of silence!

This does not imply that only grave and solemn words may be spoken. There is nothing gloomy about the religion of Christ. You look in vain through our Lord's own conversation for one gloomy sentence: he scattered only sunshine. But all his words were fitted to be helpful words. He sought to leave some gift or blessing with every one he met. He spoke words that made the careless thoughtful, that kindled hope in despairing souls, that left lights burning where all was dark before, that comforted the sorrowing, and cheered the despairing. For every one he met, he had some message; yet there was no cant in his speech. He did not go about with a sad face, uttering his messages in sanctimonious tone and phrase: his speech, like all his life, was sunny.

He is to be our model. The affectation of devoutness never ministers grace: it only caricatures religion. We are not to fill our speech with solemn phrases, and deal them out to every one we meet. Yet with Christ in our hearts, we are to seek to impart something of Christ to every one with whom we converse. There are a thousand ways of giving help. There are times when humor ministers grace, when the truest Christian help for a man is to make him laugh. Infinite are the necessities of human lives. Our feeling toward others is ever to be a strong desire to do them good. We have an errand to each one with whom we are permitted to hold even the briefest and most casual conversation. What it is, we may not know; but, if the desire be in our heart, God will use us to minister blessing in some way. Opportunities for such ministry are occurring continually. In a morning's greeting, we may put so much heart and so much Christ into phrase and tone as to make our neighbor happier all the day. In the few moments' conversation by the wayside, or during the formal call, or in the midst of the day's heat and strife, we may drop the word that will lift a burden, or strengthen a fainting heart, or inspire a new hope, or give warning of danger. We should certainly not be always flippant, talking only of trifles. There are some who never say a serious or thoughtful word. We may never see our friend again, and any passing conversation with him may be the last that we shall ever have. We should not fail, then, even in our briefest and idlest talk, to let fall at least one inspiring and helpful sentence, which may prove a blessing to the one who listens to us.

> "Only one little word,
> But it stirred the depths of a living heart;
> And there through the years and the changes of life,
> With its blessing and glory, its darkness and strife,
> The *soul* of that little word shall abide,
> And nevermore depart."

So we may leave blessings at every step of our way. Our words in season, throbbing with love, and wafted by the breath of silent prayer, shall be medicine to every heart into which any simplest sentence of our speech may fall.

CHAPTER XXI.

THE HOME CONVERSATION.

> " The angry word suppressed, the taunting thought,
> Subduing and subdued, the petty strife
> Which clouds the color of domestic life;
> The sober comfort, all the peace which springs
> From the large aggregate of little things, —
> On these small cares of daughter, wife, or friend,
> The almost sacred joys of home depend."
> HANNAH MORE.

FEW things are more important in a home than its conversation, yet there are few things to which less deliberate thought is given. We take great pains to have our house well furnished. We select our carpets and pictures with the utmost care. We send our children to school that they may become intelligent. We strive to bring into our homes the best conditions of happiness. But how often is the speech of the household left untrained and undisciplined?

The good we might do in our homes with our tongues, if we would use them to the limit of their capacity of cheer and helpfulness, it is simply impossible to state. That in most homes the best possible results from the gift of speech are not attained, is very evident. Why should so much power for blessing be wasted? Especially why should we ever pervert these gifts, and use our tongues to do evil, to give pain, to scatter seeds of bitterness? It is a sad thing when a child is born dumb; but it were better far to be born dumb, and never to have the gift of speech, than, having that gift, to employ it in speaking only sharp, unloving, or angry words.

While in all places and at all times our words shall be well chosen, and should be full of the pure and gentle spirit of Christ, there are many reasons why the home conversation, pre-eminently, should be loving. Home is the place for warmth and tenderness: it should be made the brightest and sweetest spot on earth to those who dwell within its walls. We should all carry there our very best moods, tempers, and dispositions. Especially by our speech should we seek to contribute to the enrichment of the home life, helping to make it elevating and refining, and in every way ennobling in its influence. Home should inspire every tongue to speak its most loving words, yet there is in many families a great dearth of kind speech. In some cases, there is no conversation at all worthy of the name; there are no affectionate greetings in the morning, or hearty good-nights at parting when the evening closes; the meals are eaten in silence; there are no bright fireside chats over the events and incidents of the day. A stranger might mistake the home for a deaf-and-dumb institution, or for a hotel where strangers were together only for a passing season. In other cases it were even better if silence did reign, for there are words of miserable strife and shameful quarrelling heard from day to day; husband and wife, who vowed at the marriage-altar to cherish the one the other until death, keep up an incessant petty strife of words; parents, who are commanded in the Holy Word not to provoke their children to wrath, lest they be discouraged, but to bring them up in the nurture of the Lord, scarcely ever speak to them gently and in tenderness. They seem to imagine that they are not governing their children, unless they are perpetually scolding them. They fly into a passion against them at the smallest irritation. They issue their commands to them in words and tones which would better suit the despot of a petty savage tribe than the head of a Christian household. It is not strange, that, under such "nurture," the children, instead of dwelling together in unity, with loving speech, only wrangle and quarrel, speaking only bitter words in their intercourse with one another. That there are many homes of just this type, it is idle to deny. That prayer is offered morning and evening in some of these families, only makes the truth the sadder; for it is mockery for the members of a household to rise together from their knees after morning devotion, only to begin another day of strife and bitterness.

Nothing in the home life needs to be more carefully watched and more diligently cultivated than the conversation : it should be imbued with the spirit of love. No bitter word should ever be spoken.

> " The ill-timed truth we might have kept, —
> Who knows how sharp it pierced and stung?
> The word we had not sense to say, —
> Who knows how grandly it had rung? "

The talk of husband and wife, in their intercourse together, should always be tender. Anger in word, or even in tone, should never be suffered; chiding and fault-finding should never be permitted to mar the sacredness of their speech; the warmth and tenderness of their hearts should flow out in every word that they utter the one to the other; as parents, too, in their intercourse with their children, they should never speak, save in words of Christ-like gentleness. It is a fatal mistake to suppose that children's lives can grow up into beauty in an atmosphere of strife. Harsh, angry words are to their sensitive souls what frosts are to the delicate flowers. To bring them up in the nurture of the Lord, is to bring them up as Christ himself would do; and surely that would be with infinite tenderness. The blessed influence of loving speech, day after day and month after month, it is impossible to estimate: it is like the falling of warm spring sunshine and rain on the garden. Beauty and sweetness of character are likely to come from such a home.

But home conversation needs more than love to give it its best influence: it ought to be enriched by thought. The Saviour's warning against idle words should be remembered. Every wise-hearted parent will seek to train his household to converse on subjects that will yield instruction, or tend toward refinement. The table affords an excellent opportunity for this kind of education. Three times each day the family gathers there: it is a place for cheerfulness. Simply on hygienic grounds, meals should not be eaten in silence. Bright, cheerful conversation is an excellent sauce, and a prime aid to digestion. If it prolongs the meal, and thus appears to take too much time out of the busy day, it will, in the end, add to the years by increased healthfulness and lengthened life. In any case, however, something is due to refinement, and still more is due to the culture of one's home life. The table should be made the centre of the social life of the household. There, all should appear at their best and brightest: gloom should be banished. The conversation should be sprightly and sparkling: it should consist of something besides dull and threadbare commonplaces. The idle gossip of the street is not a worthy theme for such hallowed moments.

The conversation of the table should be of a kind to interest all the members of the family; hence it should vary to suit the age and intelligence of those who form the circle. The events and occurrences of each day may with profit be spoken of and discussed; and now that the daily newspaper contains so full and faithful a summary of the world's doings and happenings, this is easy. Each one may mention the event which has specially impressed him in reading or in discussion without. Bits of refined humor should always be welcome, and all wearisome recital and dull, uninteresting discussion should be avoided.

Table-talk may be enriched, and at the same time the intelligence of all the members of the family may be advanced, by bringing out at least one new fact at each meal, to be added to the common fund of knowledge. Suppose there are two or three children at the table, varying in their ages from five to twelve. Let the father or the mother have some particular subject to introduce during the meal, which will be both interesting and profitable to the younger members of the family. It may be some historical incident, or some scientific fact, or an event in the life of some distinguished man. The subject should not be above the capacity of the younger people, for whose special benefit it is introduced, nor should the conversation be overweighted by attempting too much at one time. One single fact clearly presented, and firmly impressed so as to be remembered, is better than whole chapters of information poured out in a confused jargon on minds that to-morrow cannot recall any part of it. A little thought will show the rich possible outcome of a system like this, if faithfully followed through a series of years. If but one fact is presented at every meal, there will be a thousand things taught to the children in a year. If the subjects are wisely chosen, the fund of knowledge communicated in this way will be of no inconsiderable value. A whole system of education lies in this suggestion; for, besides the communication of important knowledge, the habit of mental activity is stimulated, interest is awakened in lines of study and research which may afterwards be followed out, tastes are improved, while the effect upon the family life is elevating and refining.

It may be objected that such a system of table-talk could not be conducted without much thought, study, and preparation on the part of parents; but if the habit once were formed, and the plan properly introduced, it would be found comparatively easy for parents of ordinary intelligence to maintain it. Books are now prepared in great numbers, giving important facts in small compass. Then, there are encyclopædias and dictionaries of various kinds. The newspapers contain every week paragraphs and articles of great value in such a course. A wise use of scissors and paste will keep scrap-books well filled with materials which can readily be made available. It will be necessary to think and plan for such a system, to choose the topics in advance, and to become familiar with the facts. This work might be shared by both parents, and thus be easy for both. That it will cost time and thought and labor ought not to be an objection, for is it not worth almost any cost to secure the benefits and advantages which would result from such a system of home instruction?

These are hints only of the almost infinite possibilities of good which lie in the home conversation. That so little is realized in most cases when so much is possible, is one of the saddest things about our current life. It may be that these suggestions shall stimulate in some families, at least, an earnest search after something better than they have yet found in their desultory and aimless conversational habits. Surely there should be no home in which, amid all the light talk that flies from busy tongues, time is not found every day in which to say at least one word that shall be instructive, suggestive, elevating, or at least, in some way, helpful.

CHAPTER XXII.

AN OLD BIBLE PORTRAIT.

It is the picture of a mother of the olden times that is before us. The story of Hannah is invested with rare interest. It is one of those narratives whose charm is their unadorned simplicity. Though living so long since, when the world was so young, this mother stands yet, in the radiant spirit of her life, in the clearness of her faith, in the devotion of her motherhood, as a model for Christian mothers in these newest ages. There are some things that grow old and out of date, but motherhood does not: it is ever the same in its duties, its responsibilities, its sacred privileges, and its possibilities of influence. The old picture is new and fresh, therefore, in every age, to every true-hearted mother who looks upon it.

For one thing, Hannah, as a mother, was

enthusiastic. She was not one of those women who think children undesirable encumbrances. She did not consider herself, in her earlier married years, particularly fortunate in being free from the cares and responsibilities of motherhood. She believed that children were blessings from the Lord, that motherhood was the highest honor possible to a woman; and she sought, reverently and very earnestly, from God, the privilege of pressing a little child to her bosom, and calling it her own. This line in the ancient picture we must not overlook in these days, when children are not always regarded as blessings from the Lord, nor even always welcomed.

For another thing, when Hannah's child came, she considered it a part of her religious duty to take care of it. Instead, therefore, of going up to Shiloh to attend all the great feasts, as she had done before, she staid at home for some time, to give personal attention to the little one that God had given her, and that was still too young to be taken with safety and comfort on such long journeys. No doubt she supposed that she was worshipping God just as acceptably in doing this as if she had gone up to all the great meetings. And who will say that she was not right? A mother's first obligations are to her children: she can have no holier or more sacred duties than those which relate to them. No amount of public religious service will atone for neglect of these. She may run to temperance and missionary meetings, and abound in all kinds of charitable activities, and may do very much good among the poor, carrying blessings to many other homes, and being a blessing to other people's children, through the Sunday school or mission school; but if she fails, meanwhile, to care for her own children, she can scarcely be commended as a faithful Christian mother. She has overlooked her first and most sacred duties, while she gives her hand and heart to those that are but secondary to her. Hannah's way evidently was the true one. A mother had better be missed in the church, and at the public meetings, than be missed in her own household. Some things must be crowded out of every earnest life, but the last thing to be crowded out of a mother's life should be the faithful and loving care of her children. The preacher may urge that every one should do something in the general work of the church, and the superintendent may appeal for teachers for the Sunday school; but the mother herself must decide whether the Master wants her to take up any religious work outside her own home. For the work there she surely is responsible; for that outside she is not responsible until the other is well done, and she has time and strength for new duties.

Another thing about Hannah was, that she looked after her own baby. She did the nursing herself. She did not go to an intelligence office, and hire a foreign woman at so much a week, and then commit her tender child to her care, that she herself might have a "free foot" for parties and calls and operas, and social and religious duties. She was old-fashioned enough to prefer to nurse her own child. She does not seem to have felt it any great personal deprivation to be kept at home rather closely for a year or two on that account: she even appears to have thought it a high honor, and a distinguished privilege, to be a mother, and to do with her own hands a mother's duties. And when we think what this child that she nursed became in after-years, what the outcome was of all her pains, self-denials, and toils, it certainly looks as if Hannah was right. It is not likely she ever regretted, when she saw her son in the prime and splendor of his power and usefulness, that she had missed a few parties and other social privileges in nursing and caring for him in his tender infancy. If any thing even half so good comes ordinarily out of faithful mothering, there are certainly few occupations open to women, even in these advanced nineteenth-century days, which will yield such satisfactory results in the end as the wise and true bringing up of children. Many women are sighing for distinction in the professions, or as authors, or artists, or singers; but, after all, is there any distinction so noble, so honorable, so worthy, and so enduring as that which a true mother wins when she has brought up a son who takes his place in the ranks of good and true men? Could Mary, the mother of Jesus, have found any mission, in any century, greater than that of nursing and caring for the holy Child that was laid in her arms? Or, if that example be too high, could the mothers of Moses, of Samuel, of Augustine, of Washington, have done more for the world if they had devoted themselves to art, or poetry, or music, or a profession?

Perhaps Hannah was right; and, if so, the old-fashioned motherhood is better than the new, and the mother herself is her own child's best nurse. A hired woman may be very skilful; but surely she cannot be the best one to mould the soul of the child, and waken and draw out its powers and affections. The mother may, by employing such a substitute, be left free to pursue the fashionable round of dining and dressing, of amusement and social engagements; but what is coming meanwhile of the tender, immortal life at home in the nursery, thus left practically motherless, to be nurtured and trained by a hireling stranger? And what comes besides of the holy mission of motherhood, which the birth of every child lays upon her who gave it life? A recent writer, referring to this subject, asks, "Is there any malfeasance of office in these days of dishonor like unto this? Our women crowd the churches, to draw the inspiration of religion for their daily duties, and then prove recreant to the first of all fidelities, the most solemn of all responsibilities. We hear fashionable young mothers boast that they are not tied down to their nurseries, but are free to keep in the old gay life, as though there were no shame to the soul of womanhood therein." Such a boast is one of the saddest confessions a mother could make. The great want of this age is mothers who will live with their own children, and throw over their tender lives all the mighty power of their own rich, warm, loving natures. If we can have a generation of Hannahs, we shall then have a generation of Samuels growing up under their wise, devoted nurture.

There is one other feature in this old-time mother that should not be overlooked. She nursed her child for the Lord. From the very first she looked upon him as God's child, not hers, and considered herself as only God's nurse, whose duty it was to bring up the child for a holy life and service. It is easy to see what a dignity and splendor this gave to the whole toilsome round of motherly tasks and duties which the successive days brought to her hand. This was God's child that she was nursing, and she was bringing him up for the Lord's service in two worlds. Nothing ever seemed drudgery: no duty to her little one was hard or distasteful, with this thought ever glowing in her heart. Need any woman have loftier or more powerful inspiration for toil and self-forgetfulness than this?

And is there any mother who may not have the same inspiration as she goes through her round of commonplace nursery tasks? Was Samuel God's child in any higher sense when Hannah was nursing him than are the little ones that lie in the arms of thousands of mothers to-day? In every mother's ears, when a baby is laid in her bosom, there is spoken by the breath of the Lord the holy whisper, if she but have ears to hear the divine voice, "Take this child, and nurse it *for me.*" All children belong to God, and he wants them brought up for pure and noble lives, and for holy missions. Every mother is, by the very lot of motherhood when it falls upon her, consecrated to the sacred service of nursing, moulding, and training an infant life for God. Hannah understood this, and found her task full of glory. But how many, even among Christian mothers, fail to understand it, and, unsustained by a consciousness of the dignity and blessedness of their high calling, look upon its duties and self-denials as painful tasks, a round of toilsome, wearisome drudgery?

It will be well worth while for every mother to sit down quietly beside Hannah, and try to learn her secret. It will change the humblest nursery into a holy sanctuary, and transform the commonest, lowliest duties of motherhood into services as splendid as those the radiant angels perform before the Father's face.

CHAPTER XXIII.

SORROW IN CHRISTIAN HOMES.

> " Men die, but sorrow never dies:
> The corroding years divide in vain,
> And the wide world is knit with ties
> Of common brotherhood in pain."
>
> SUSAN COOLIDGE.

SOONER or later, sorrow comes to every home. No conditions of wealth or culture or social standing, or even of religion, can exclude it. When two young people come from the marriage-altar, and set up their new home, it seems to them that its joy never can be disturbed, that grief can never reach their hearts in that charmed spot. For a few years, perhaps, their fond dream remains unbroken. The flowers bloom into still softer beauty and richer fragrance; the music continues light and joyous, with no minor chords; the circle is unbroken; child-lives grow up in the tender atmosphere, blessing the home with their love and lovableness; the household life flows on softly and smoothly, like a river, gathering in breadth and depth as it flows. In other homes, all about, there are sorrows, — bereavements, or griefs that are sorer than bereavements, — but amid these desolations of the dreams of other households, this one remains untouched, like an oasis in the desert; but not forever does the exemption continue. There comes a day when the strange messenger of sorrow stands at the door, nor waits for bidding and welcome, but enters, and lays his withering hand on some sweet flower.

The first experience of grief is very sore: its suddenness and strangeness add to its terribleness. What seemed so impossible yesterday, has become a fearful reality to-day. The dear one whom we held so securely, as we thought that we never could lose her, is gone now, and answers no more to our call. It seems to us that we never can be comforted, that we never can enjoy life again, since the one who made for us so much of the gladness of life has been taken away. The time of the first sorrow is to every life a most critical point, a time of great danger. The way is new and untried, one over which the feet have never passed before. At no other point, therefore, is wise and loving guidance more needed. Many lives are wrecked on the hidden reefs and the low, dangerous rocks that skirt the shores of sorrow's sea. Many persons find in grief an enemy only, to whom they refuse to be reconciled, and with whom they contend in fierce strife, receiving only injury and harm to themselves in the unavailing conflict.

An impression prevails, that sorrow is in itself a blessing in its influence, that it always makes purer and holier and better the lives that it touches; but this is not true. Sorrow has in itself no cleansing efficacy, as some suppose, by which it removes from sinful lives their blemishes and stains. The same fire which refines the gold destroys the flowers. Sorrow is a fire, which in God's hand is designed to purify the lives of his people, but which, unblessed, produces only desolation. It depends on the relation of the sufferer to Christ, as friend or enemy, and on the reception given to grief, whether it leave good or ill where it enters; but in a Christian home, where the love of Christ dwells and holds sway, sorrow should always leave a benediction. It should be received as God's own messenger; and we should welcome it, and listen for the divine message it bears.

For God's angels do not always come to us, as we are apt to imagine them coming, in radiant dress, with smiling face and gentle voice. Thus artists paint them in their pictures. Thus we fancy them in their ministries. We think of them as possessing rare and wondrous loveliness; and so, no doubt, they do as they appear before God, and serve in his presence. There is no unloveliness in any angel-face in heaven. No angel has features of sternness; but, as these celestial messengers come to earth on their ministries, they appear ofttimes in forms that appal, and fill the trembling heart with terror and alarm. Yet ofttimes it is when they come in these very forms that they bring their sweetest messages and their best blessings.

"All God's angels come to us disguised, —
Sorrow and sickness, poverty and death,
One after other lift their frowning masks,
And we behold the seraph's face beneath,
All radiant with the glory and the calm
Of having looked upon the face of God."

Wherever God's messenger of sorrow is thus received in a Christian home, with welcome even amid tears and pain, it will leave a blessing of peace, and will make the home sweeter, tenderer, heavenlier. We speak of love as the atmosphere in which the home reaches its best development in the direction of happiness, as in summer warmth the flowers unfold their rarest beauty and sweetest fragrance; but really no home ever attains its highest blessedness and joy, and its fullest richness of life, until in some way sorrow enters its door. Even the home love, like certain autumn fruits, does not ripen into its sweetest tenderness until the frosts of trial have touched it. When a green log of wood is laid on the andirons, on a winter evening, and the fire begins to play about the log, a weird, plaintive music comes from the wood. A poet would tell you, that, while the tree stood in the forest, the birds sat amid its branches, and sang there, and that the notes of their songs hid away in the tree. Then he would tell you that the music you now hear from the log as it burns, is this bird-minstrelsy, which has remained imprisoned in the wood until brought out by the hot flames. The poet's thought is only a fancy, but it well illustrates a truth concerning the life of a Christian home, which is worth pondering and remembering. In the sunny days of joy, the bird-notes of gladness are sung all about us, and sink away into our hearts, and hide there. The lessons, the influences, the tender impressions, the peace, and the beautiful things of quiet, happy, prosperous years, fall upon our lives, as the sunbeams and rain-showers fall upon the fields all the long autumn and winter and early spring, and seem to be lost. There appears but little to show for so much absorption of brightness and blessing. Our lives do not appear to yield the measure of joy they should yield. Then the flames of trial are kindled; and, in the heat of suffering, the long-gathering and long-slumbering music is set free, and flows out.

Many of the world's best things have been born of affliction. The sweetest songs ever sung on earth have been called out by suffering. The richest blessings that we enjoy have come to us out of the fire. The good things we inherit from the past are the purchase of suffering and sacrifice. Our redemption comes from Gethsemane and Calvary. We get heaven through Christ's tears and blood. Whatever is richest and most valuable in life anywhere has been in the fire. Our love for one another may be strong and true in the sunny days, but it never reaches its holiest and fullest expression until pain has touched our hearts, and called out the hidden treasures of affliction. Even the love of a mother for her child, deep and pure as it is, never reaches its full wondrousness of devotion and sacrifice until the child suffers, and the mother bends over it in yearning and solicitude. The same is true of all the home loves: the best and divinest qualities in them come out only in the fires. The household that has endured sorrow in the true spirit of love and faith, emerges from it undestroyed, untarnished, with purer, tenderer affections, with less of passion, of selfishness, and of earthliness. When husband and wife stand together beside their dead child, they are drawn to each other as never before: their common grief is sacramental. Children that remain are dearer to parents after one has been taken. Brothers and sisters grow more thoughtful and patient in their mutual intercourse when the home circle has been broken. There is in an empty chair in a Christian home a wondrous power to soften the asperities of nature, and refine all the affections and feelings. The cloud of grief that hangs over a household, like the summer cloud above the fields and gardens, leaves blessings.

> " Is it raining, little flower?
>   Be glad of rain.
> Too much sun would wither thee.
>   'Twill shine again.
> The sky is very black, 'tis true,
> But just behind it shines the blue.

> Art thou weary, tender heart?
> Be glad of pain;
> In sorrow sweetest things will grow
> As flowers in rain.
> God watches, and thou wilt have sun
> When clouds their perfect work have done."

But how may we make sure of the benedictions that sorrow brings? Even the gospel is the savor of death to those who reject it; and sorrow, though it be God's evangel, ofttimes comes and goes away again, leaving no heavenly gift. How must we treat this dark-robed messenger, if we would receive the heavenly blessings it bears in its hands? We must welcome it, even in our trembling and tears, as sent from God. We must believe that it comes from our Father, and that, coming from him, it is a messenger of love to us, bearing a true blessing for us, though it be a loss or a pain. We must ask for the message which God has sent us in the affliction, and listen to it as we would to a message of gladness. It has some mission to us, or some gift from heaven. Some golden fruit lies hidden in the rough husk. Some bit of gold in us God designs to be set free from its dross by this fire. There is some radiant height beyond this dark valley, to which he wants to lead us. Christ himself accepted and endured with loving submission the bitter sorrow of his cross, because he saw the joy set before him and waiting beyond the sorrow. In the same way, we should accept our griefs, because they are but the shaded gateways to peace and blessedness. If we cannot get through the gateways, we cannot get the radiant joys that wait beyond. Not to be able to take from our Father's hand the seed of pain, is to miss the fruits of blessing which can grow from no other sowing. If we are wise, we will give sorrow as cordial a welcome as joy; for it is from the same loving hand, and brings gifts as good and golden.

We must remember, that it is in the home where Christ himself dwells, that sorrow unlocks its heavenly treasures. A Christless home receives none of them. Those who shut their doors on Christ, shut out all blessedness, and, when the lamps of earthly joy go out, are left in utter darkness. A wise forethought will make sure of the hopes and comforts of a personal interest in Christ, and of having him as guest in the sunny days, that, when the shadow of night falls, the stars of bright hope may shine out.

CHAPTER XXIV.

DEALING WITH OUR SINS.

It takes courage to look our own sins in the face, and to deal with them as we would counsel another to do, if the sins were his. It was one of the old psalm-writers who said, "I thought on my ways." It is not likely that even he found it an easy thing to do. It is usually very much harder to think on our own ways than on other people's: most of us do quite enough of the latter. We keep a magnifying-glass to inspect our neighbor's life, a high-power microscope to hunt for specks in his character; but too often we forget to use our glasses on ourselves, or, if we do, we reverse them, and thus minify every spot and imperfection. The Pharisee in the temple confessed a great many sins, but they were his neighbor's sins and the publican's sins: he made no confession of sin for himself. Most of us are in the same danger. We like to think of our ways when they are good, — it flatters our vanity to be able to approve and commend ourselves; but, when our conduct has not been particularly satisfactory, we like to turn our back upon it, and solace ourselves meanwhile by thinking on our neighbor's evil ways. And here, strange to say, it seems to please many of us best to find things we cannot approve or commend. One of the last lessons of Christian charity which most of us learn, is to rejoice with others in their attainments of character, and to be pained and grieved when we find blemishes and stains in their lives.

But it is a brave thing for a man to say, "I will think upon my own ways," and to say it when he knows his ways have not been good and right, but wrong. It is an excellent thing for us to turn our lenses in upon our own hearts, in order to see if our own ways are right. This should always be our first duty. We should take heed to ourselves before we try to look after the mistakes of others, and point them out. There is only one person in all the world for whose ways any of us are really personally responsible, for whose life any one will be required to give account, — and that is one's self. Other people's wrong ways may pain us, and offend our sense of right; and it is our duty to do all we can, in the spirit of Christ, to lead our neighbors into better ways: but, after all, when we stand before God's judgment-seat, the only one person in the whole world for whom any of us will have to be judged will be one's self. Certainly it is most important, then, that we give earnest heed to ourselves and our own ways in this world.

Retrospect has a strange power. As we look back upon our ways, they do not appear to us as they did when we were passing through them. Things that seemed hard and painful at the time, now, as we look back upon them, appear lovely and radiant. There are experiences in most lives that at the time seemed to be calamities, but in the end prove rich blessings. Then, there is another class, — things which appeared attractive and enjoyable at the time, which afterward look repulsive and abhorrent. This is true of all wrong actions, all deeds wrought under the influence of the evil passions. At the time, they give a thrill of pleasure; but when the emotion has passed, and the wrong-doer turns and looks back at what he has done, it seems horrible in his eyes. The retrospect fills him with disgust and loathing.

To look at one's ways when they have been wrong is not by any means a pleasant thing to do. Such looks, if honest, will produce deep sorrow. It is well that it should be so,—that regret should grow into sore pain, until it has burned into our hearts the lessons which we ought to learn from our follies and sins. But pain and regret should not be all. The Scriptures speak of the sorrow of the world which works death. This is a sorrow which passes away like the morning cloud or the early dew, leaving no impression, working no improvement, or the sorrow which ends only in despair. Godly sorrow is the pain for sins which leads to repentance. The prodigal in the far-off land thought on his ways, and, in his shame, hid his face in his hands, and wept bitter tears over the ruin he had made of his life. But he did more than weep: he rose and went straight home to his father. No matter how badly one has failed, the noble thing to do is, not to sit down and waste other years in grieving over the lost years. Weeping in the darkness of despair amends nothing. The only truly wise thing to do is to rise, and save what remains. Because ten hours out of the allotted twelve are lost, shall we sit down and waste the other two in unavailing grief over the ten? Had we not better use the two that are left in doing what we can to retrieve the consequences of our past folly? "We have lost the battle," said Napoleon; "but," drawing his watch from his pocket, "it is only two o'clock, and we have time to fight and win another:" and the sun went down on a victorious army. No young person, especially, should ever yield to despair; for in youth, there is yet too wide a margin to blot with the confession of defeat and failure. Even old age, with a whole lifetime behind it wasted, is not hopeless in a world on which Christ's cross stood. A few moments of sincere penitence and true repentance are enough in which to creep to Christ's feet, and find pardon. The divine mercy is so great, that no one need perish, though his sins be as scarlet. Then, though the life be so utterly wrecked, its glory so destroyed, its powers so wasted, that on earth it can never be any thing, even when saved, but a shattered ruin, it may still become radiant and beautiful in the blessed immortality which Christian faith reveals. Life does not end at the grave. Its path sweeps on into the eternal years, and there will be time enough then to retrieve all the wasted past. Some one speaks of heaven as the place where God makes over souls. Even lives wasted and marred on earth, turning to Christ only in the late evening-time, may find mercy, and in heaven's long, blessed day be made over into grace and beauty.

But no careful seaman will run his ship twice on the same rock or reef. Even a child will not be likely to put his hand a second time into the flame. We should learn by experience in living, and should not repeat the same folly, mistake, or sin over and over. Every error we make should be marked, and never made again. Thus we should use our very failures as stepping-stones by which to climb to a higher, better life. Nothing comes of thinking on our ways if we do not turn from whatever we find to be wrong. Godly sorrow works repentance. A few tears amount to nothing if one goes on to-morrow in the same old paths. Some one says, "The true science of blundering consists in never making the same mistake twice." This rule applies to sins as well as to mistakes. The true science of living is never to commit the same sin a second time.

But even this falls short. We are not saved by negatives. We can never go to heaven by merely turning from wrong ways. True repentance leads to Christ, and into his ways. It is the man who forsakes his wicked ways, and his wicked thoughts, and returns to the Lord, who is abundantly pardoned. No matter how black the sin when there is this kind of repentance. Even Christ does not undo the wrong past, and make that which has been done as though it had never been done. It never can be made true that the thief did not once steal; but grace may so make over a marred life, that, where the blemish was, some special beauty may appear. "The oyster mends its shell with a pearl." Where the ugly wound was, there comes, with the healing, not a scar, but a pearl. The same is true in human souls when divine grace heals the wounds of sins. Sins that we truly repent of become pearls in the character. It is the experience of all who grow into Christ-like nobleness, that many of the golden lines of their later lives have been wrought out through their regrets and their repentings of wrong-doings.

Some one says, "The besetting sin may become the guardian angel. Let us thank God that we can say it! Yes, this sin that has sent me weary-hearted to bed, and desperate in heart to morning work, can be conquered. I do not say annihilated, but, better than that, conquered, captured, and transfigured into a friend; so that

I, at last, shall say, 'My temptation has become my strength; for to the very fight with it I owe my force.'"

"We rise by the things that are under feet;
  By what we have mastered of good or gain;
  By the pride deposed, and the passion slain,
And the vanquished ills that we hourly meet."

An old man sat thinking, one day, about his past, recounting to himself his mistakes and follies, and regretting them, wishing he had never committed them, and that there was some way of undoing them. He took his pen, and on a sheet of paper made a list of twenty things in his life of which he was ashamed, and was about to seize an imaginary sponge, and rub them all out of his biography. He was thinking how much more beautiful his character would have been at the close of his years if these wrong things had never been committed. But to his amazement, as he thought of wiping out these evil things, he found, that, if there were any golden threads of beauty running through his life, they had been woven into the web by the regrets he had felt over his wrong-doings; and that, if he should wipe out these wrong acts, he would at the same time destroy the fairest lines of nobleness and worth in his present character. He learned in his meditation that he had gotten all his best things out of his errors, with the painful regrets, the wise lessons, the true repentings, and the new life, which followed.

There is a deep truth in this record of experience: it is, that even our mistakes and sins, if we leave them, and find our way to Christ, will be transmuted into growth and the upbuilding of character. "We can so deal with the past, that we can make it give up to us virtue and wisdom." "We can make wrong the seed of right and righteousness; we can transmute error into wisdom; we can make sorrow bloom into a thousand forms, like fragrant flowers." If we truly repent of our sins, then, where they grew with their thorns and poison-seeds, there will be in our lives trees and plants of beauty with sweet flowers and rich fruits. Our very falls become new births to our souls, if we rise again, and, in lowly penitence and sincere return, creep to the feet of Christ. His tender grace heals the wounds our sins have made, and restores our lives to strength and beauty; but it must never be forgotten, that Christ alone can thus save us from our sins, and transmute their evil into good. This wondrous alchemy exists only in the Saviour's cross and blood. Left to itself, sin works death; but, brought to Christ, the poison is destroyed, and death is changed to life. Longfellow says of the power of Christ's look after we have sinned, —

> " One look of that pale, suffering face
> Will make us feel the deep disgrace
>   Of weakness :
> We shall be sifted till the strength
> Of self-conceit be changed at length
>   To meekness.
>
> Wounds of the soul, though healed, will ache;
> The reddening scars remain, and make
>   Confession ;
> Lost innocence returns no more :
> We are not what we were before
>   Transgression.

DEALING WITH OUR SINS.

> But noble souls, through dust and heat,
> Rise from disaster and defeat
>   The stronger,
> And, conscious still of the divine
> Within them, lie on earth supine
>   No longer."

In every life, there are mistakes and sins. The holiest do not live perfectly. The strongest are liable to fall in sudden and unexpected temptation. The wisest will commit grave errors and follies at some time. We should know well in such cases how to deal with our sins. They must not be simply self-condoned, and left lying in the path behind us, while we hurry on; nor must they bring despair to our hearts as we sorrow over them; they must be sincerely and heartily repented of, and forgiveness for them sought at the feet of Him we have offended and grieved. Then we must rise from disaster and defeat stronger, purer, nobler, through Christ victorious over our own sins, and a conqueror over our own defeat.

"Yet, my soul, look not behind thee!
Thou hast work to do at last:
Let the brave toil of the present
Overarch thy crumbling past;
Build thy great acts high and higher,
Build them on the conquered sod
Where thy weakness first fell bleeding,
Where thy first prayer was to God."

www.ingramcontent.com/pod-product-compliance
Lightning Source LLC
Chambersburg PA
CBHW032136230426
43672CB00011B/2357